D1091607

"... Anderson's ... David Hume is an uncommonly successful introduction, explanation, and assessment of the work of one of the most influential authors of the last three hundred years. Anderson's account of Hume's project, method, and principal conclusions is clear, accessible, and philosophically perceptive. In a remarkably short space, Anderson gives a very strong overview of Hume that makes Hume's importance easy to understand. His assessment of the success of Hume's overall project and individual assertions is rich, biblically serious, consistently Reformed, and likely to edify readers regardless of their previous exposure to Hume's works. Although Anderson sometimes extends his analysis further than space allows him to justify, the work on the whole is a model of Christian philosophical analysis. He summarizes Hume fairly, assesses Hume's success relative to both Hume's own assumptions and the truth of Scripture, and shows how Hume's work points toward important insights about the limits of fallen natural reason."

—**Bill Davis**, Professor of Philosophy, Covenant College; former member, Hume Society

"The skepticism of David Hume has frightened many who have sought to follow Christ. But James Anderson's book shows that it is the followers of Hume who should be frightened. Anderson presents an account of Hume that is accurate and comprehensive, yet concise. It is easy to follow. And it shows clearly where Hume went wrong, and how his errors illumine the biblical alternative. Hume fell into skepticism because he failed to think God's thoughts after him."

—**John M. Frame**, Professor of Systematic Theology and Philosophy Emeritus, Reformed Theological Seminary, Orlando

"James Anderson's book on David Hume is a masterly summary and critique of one of the most important and influential philosophers in modern Western history. With clarity and insight, Anderson presents the overall structure of Hume's philosophical work, as well as devastating criticisms of Hume's epistemological project. Once read and grasped, this book will provide the context and proper, Christian critique for anyone wanting to pursue further study in Hume, or in Western thought since Hume. I am glad to have Anderson's book in my library."

—**K. Scott Oliphint**, Dean of Faculty, Professor of Apologetics and Systematic Theology, Westminster Theological Seminary

"As James Anderson rightly argues, the reach and influence of Hume's philosophy is almost unparalleled in the modern West, not only standing as a salient and powerful articulation of empiricism in its own right but decisively influencing other great thinkers such as Kant, Hegel, and Marx. Anderson's introduction to Hume's thought is concise but not curtailed, straightforward but not simplistic. To my eyes the book's greatest value is in the second half, where Anderson carefully marshals a Reformed response to Hume. Weaving together arguments from Cornelius Van Til and Alvin Plantinga, he shows how Hume's arguments are won or lost in their axioms: naturalism is Hume's starting point, not his conclusion, and he sets the bar of knowledge so high that even his own philosophical principles fail to clear it. This is a lively volume, crackling with some memorable turns of phrase: I particularly enjoyed the description of logical positivism as 'decapitation as a cure for a headache,' and the deft summary that although 'the modern conception of religion as a strictly private matter can be laid at the feet of Kant,' yet those feet 'were shod by Hume.' There is much of profit here both for students new to Hume and for scholars wanting to explore a Reformed response to his influential philosophy. It is, I suspect, harder to write a short book on Hume than a long one, and harder to write for those new to Humean philosophy than for old hands. Anderson has accomplished this task with aplomb in this sturdy and very accessible gem of a volume."

—**Christopher Watkin**, Senior Lecturer in French Studies, Monash University, Melbourne, Australia

Praise for the Great Thinkers Series

"After a long eclipse, intellectual history is back. We are becoming aware, once again, that ideas have consequences. The importance of P&R Publishing's leadership in this trend cannot be overstated. The series Great Thinkers: Critical Studies of Minds That Shape Us is a tool that I wish I had possessed when I was in college and early in my ministry. The scholars examined in this well-chosen group have shaped our minds and habits more than we know. Though succinct, each volume is rich, and displays a balance between what Christians ought to value and what they ought to reject. This is one of the happiest publishing events in a long time."

—**William Edgar**, Professor of Apologetics, Westminster Theological Seminary

"When I was beginning my studies of theology and philosophy during the 1950s and '60s, I profited enormously from P&R's Modern Thinkers Series. Here were relatively short books on important philosophers and theologians such as Nietzsche, Dewey, Van Til, Barth, and Bultmann by scholars of Reformed conviction such as Clark, Van Riessen, Ridderbos, Polman, and Zuidema. These books did not merely summarize the work of these thinkers; they were serious critical interactions. Today, P&R is resuming and updating the series, now called Great Thinkers. The new books, on people such as Aquinas, Hume, Nietzsche, Derrida, and Foucault, are written by scholars who are experts on these writers. As before, these books are short—around 100 pages. They set forth accurately the views of the thinkers under consideration, and they enter into constructive dialogue, governed by biblical and Reformed convictions. I look forward to the release of all the books being planned and to the good influence they will have on the next generation of philosophers and theologians."

    —**John M. Frame**, Professor of Systematic Theology and Philosophy Emeritus, Reformed Theological Seminary, Orlando

David

HUME

GREAT THINKERS

A Series

Series Editor
Nathan D. Shannon

AVAILABLE IN THE GREAT THINKERS SERIES

Thomas Aquinas, by K. Scott Oliphint
Francis Bacon, by David C. Innes
Richard Dawkins, by Ransom Poythress
Jacques Derrida, by Christopher Watkin
Michel Foucault, by Christopher Watkin
G. W. F. Hegel, by Shao Kai Tseng
David Hume, by James N. Anderson
Karl Marx, by William D. Dennison
Karl Rahner, by Camden M. Bucey

FORTHCOMING

Karl Barth, by Lane G. Tipton
Gilles Deleuze, by Christopher Watkin
Immanuel Kant, by Shao Kai Tseng
Friedrich Nietzsche, by Carl R. Trueman
Adam Smith, by Jan van Vliet

David

HUME

James N. Anderson

P&R
PUBLISHING
P.O. BOX 817 • PHILLIPSBURG • NEW JERSEY 08865-0817

© 2019 by James N. Anderson

All rights reserved. No part of this book may be reproduced, stored in a retrieval system, or transmitted in any form or by any means—electronic, mechanical, photocopy, recording, or otherwise—except for brief quotations for the purpose of review or comment, without the prior permission of the publisher, P&R Publishing Company, P.O. Box 817, Phillipsburg, New Jersey 08865–0817.

ISBN: 978-1-62995-279-6 (pbk)
ISBN: 978-1-62995-280-2 (ePub)
ISBN: 978-1-62995-281-9 (Mobi)

Printed in the United States of America

Library of Congress Cataloging-in-Publication Data

Names: Anderson, James N., 1973- author.
Title: David Hume / James N. Anderson.
Description: Phillipsburg : P&R Publishing, 2019. | Series: Great thinkers | Includes index.
Identifiers: LCCN 2019001924| ISBN 9781629952796 (pbk.) | ISBN 9781629952802 (epub) | ISBN 9781629952819 (mobi)
Subjects: LCSH: Hume, David, 1711-1776. | Christian philosophy.
Classification: LCC B1498 .A53 2019 | DDC 192--dc23
LC record available at https://lccn.loc.gov/2019001924

To my parents, David and Judith

CONTENTS

SERIES INTRODUCTION

Amid the rise and fall of nations and civilizations, the influence of a few great minds has been profound. Some of these remain relatively obscure, even as their thought shapes our world; others have become household names. As we engage our cultural and social contexts as ambassadors and witnesses for Christ, we must identify and test against the Word those thinkers who have so singularly formed the present age.

The Great Thinkers series is designed to meet the need for critically assessing the seminal thoughts of these thinkers. Great Thinkers hosts a colorful roster of authors analyzing primary source material against a background of historical contextual issues, and providing rich theological assessment and response from a Reformed perspective.

Each author was invited to meet a threefold goal, so that each Great Thinkers volume is, first, *academically informed*. The brevity of Great Thinkers volumes sets a premium on each author's command of the subject matter and on the secondary discussions that have shaped each thinker's influence. Our authors identify the most influential features of their thinkers' work and address them with precision and insight. Second, the series maintains a high standard of *biblical and theological faithfulness*. Each volume stands on an epistemic commitment to "the whole counsel of God" (Acts 20:27), and is thereby equipped for fruitful critical engagement. Finally, Great Thinkers texts are *accessible*, not burdened with jargon or unnecessarily difficult vocabulary. The goal is to inform and equip the reader as effectively as possible through clear writing, relevant analysis, and incisive, constructive critique. My hope is that this series will distinguish itself by striking with biblical faithfulness and the riches of the Reformed tradition at the central nerves of culture, cultural history, and intellectual heritage.

Bryce Craig, president of P&R Publishing, deserves hearty thanks for his initiative and encouragement in setting the series in motion and seeing it through. Many thanks as well to P&R's director of academic development, John Hughes, who has assumed, with cool efficiency, nearly every role on the production side of each volume. The Rev. Mark Moser carried much of the burden in the initial design of the series, acquisitions, and editing of the first several volumes. And the expert participation of Amanda Martin, P&R's editorial director, was essential at every turn. I have long admired P&R Publishing's commitment, steadfast now for over eighty-five years, to publishing excellent books promoting biblical understanding and cultural awareness, especially in the area of Christian apologetics. Sincere thanks to P&R, to these fine brothers and sisters, and to several others not mentioned here for the opportunity to serve as editor of the Great Thinkers series.

Nathan D. Shannon
Seoul, Korea

FOREWORD

Every momentous shift in Western philosophy and science had its origin in founding voices that blazed new ways of thinking. They isolated and refuted weaknesses of preceding thought. They proposed radically different modes of reasoning. Identifying such individuals for the many forms of Enlightenment that crisscrossed Europe in the seventeenth and eighteenth centuries invites intense discussion. But two disciplines stand out as crucial for the optimism that marked the Enlightenment era—science and philosophy. Both began with individuals who published their groundbreaking works within twenty years of each other— Francis Bacon, an Englishman who penned *Novum Organum* in 1620, and René Descartes, a Frenchman who wrote *Meditations on First Philosophy* in 1641. As a result of their influence, England became associated with the school of empiricism and scientific experimentation and the Continent became coupled with philosophical rationalism.

How alike and yet different were these two heralds of modern thought? Both men were Renaissance-like figures whose interests spanned several intellectual disciplines. Bacon's contributions included works in politics, law, literature, and philosophy. Most significantly, he pleaded for a new era of science, which led to his being named the "father of modern science." His reputation was owed not to his role as a practicing scientist but to his imploring his peers to begin experimenting. Descartes' efforts spanned philosophy, science, and mathematics. He laid the foundation for analytical geometry and calculus. But most importantly, he sounded the opening salvo for a new, modern rationalist philosophy.

Despite similarities of initiating new methods in their disciplines, Bacon and Descartes differed sharply. Profoundly dissatisfied with past philosophers' reliance on previous authorities, Descartes refocused the philosophic quest for certainty. He cited several fields of intellectual inquiry for their past failures, including science for its forays in alchemy and astrology; and institutional religions for their wildly differing confessions, sacraments, and devotional practices. None of these fields yielded the certainty that ought to characterize the modern quest for knowledge. (An important caveat, however, is frequently overlooked by historians of philosophy. In the rush to vaunt the secular cast to modern thinking, historians often fail to acknowledge that Descartes maintained a deep devotion to his Roman Catholic faith until his death.)

Philosophy fared no better with the plethora of approaches to knowledge extending back to ancient Greece. Descartes would have belittled Alfred North Whitehead's famous dictum, "The safest general characterization of the European philosophical tradition is that it consists of a series of footnotes to Plato." For a solution to the undecidedness of previous efforts, Descartes turned the human mind inward—a "subjective turn" away from sensory experience, which can only deceive. After this initial doubting, he centered his attention on ideas that are innate to the mind—ideas that are so clear and distinct that they cannot be doubted. Greatly abbreviated, Descartes' epistemological certitude lay in arriving at the certainty of the existing self. From this subjective starting point, he proceeded to prove the existence of God, which in turn served as his bridge to the existence of the material world. The whole process could be distilled this way: *dubito, cogito, ergo sum* ("I doubt, I think, therefore I am").

While Descartes' method for a revolutionary new basis of thinking lay in epistemology, Bacon's proposal for a *Novum Organum*—a new body of knowledge—was for a fresh start in science. *Novum Organum* was not a treatise but a series of aphorisms offered in the spirit of inquiry based on experimentation. Science as then practiced utilized a deductive method in which the Aristotelian worldview and the Ptolemaic cosmos were accepted as axiomatic for scientific thinking. Unfortunately, contended Bacon, such a method does not help scientists achieve new knowledge. In sum, no one was experimenting. Aphorism 36 stated that "we must force [scientists] for a while to lay their notions aside and begin to familiarize themselves with facts." Scientists should replace centuries of a deductive method and substitute in its place an empirical method—inductive investigation. Bacon's seminal work was but a part of his larger project, an unfinished *summa*—*Instauratio Magna*—a comprehensive blueprint encompassing all the various sciences that would enable mankind to master nature, which had been lost since the fall of Adam.

Descartes' *Meditations* and Bacon's *Novum Organum* opened the floodgates for modernity in philosophy and science. If moderns followed their leads, mankind would forge new beginnings. So novel were their proposals that they were demanding that people *think again for the first time*—an obvious logical impossibility but nevertheless absolutely necessary enterprise simply because past eras had not offered the certainty and progress that modernity could deliver. Within a century, Spinoza's monism,

Leibniz's *Monadologie*, and Malebranch's occasionalism would demonstrate the various forms that rationalism would take. And in science, among other advances, Galileo's experiments would demonstrate the truth of Copernicus's hypothesis of the heliocentric universe.

The modern era's penchant for new philosophies and garnering of facts produced a mood of optimism relatively unrivaled in human history. A little more than a century later, Marquis de Condorcet would propose his *Sketch for a Historical Picture of the Progress of the Human Mind*. He foresaw the abolition of inequality between the nations and growth of equality within nations. He predicted that new instruments and machines would only add to human strength. Social problems would disappear, as would disease and poverty. Carl Becker later characterized this era in *The Heavenly City of the Eighteenth-Century Philosophers*. To the Enlightenment philosophers, the vision of a heavenly city—which for Augustine would be achieved only by God's sovereign, supernatural consummation of history—would be realized by human means within history.

Into this milieu we situate David Hume, the subject of James Anderson's fine book. Over against Cartesian rationalism, John Locke launched an empiricist epistemological rejoinder. Knowledge did not originate from ideas innate to the human mind. Instead, the mind was *tabula rasa*—a blank slate. Ideas arose in the mind from sense experience. Hume's contribution to the empiricist hegemony in Britain consisted in taking the foundational premises of Locke's empiricism to their logical conclusion. In so doing, however, rather than achieving the certainty that Enlightenment thinkers sought in all disciplines by their new methods, Hume's philosophy devolved into skepticism. James Anderson's careful and equally precise examination of Hume's thought in chapters appropriately entitled "Hume's Philosophical Project," "Hume's Naturalistic Ethics," and "Hume's Religious

Skepticism" demonstrates the brilliance of Humean thought, but also its critical weaknesses. If the philosophical quest begins with our subjective impressions alone, not only can we not know causality, we cannot know God or moral obligation or even our own selves.

Reformed readers will agree that despite the skeptical shadow that Hume's thought cast over modern thought, he made several valuable contributions. He demonstrated that rational method alone (for example, the popular cosmological argument for the existence of God) utterly fails. Hume challenges the notion that it is possible to establish a priori any necessary truths about causation. Perhaps things can come into existence on their own without any cause. On the basis of reason alone, even the use of analogies does not produce epistemological certainty. Why infer an infinite God as the cause of a finite cosmos? Anderson states Hume's point succinctly: "He who lives by the analogical sword will also die by it." Is not the inference of a single infinite, single spiritual being as the cause of a multitude of finite material objects out of all proportion? Likewise, Hume refuted the often-used *is/ought* fallacy in ethics.

Anderson details how Immanuel Kant, having been awakened by Hume from his "dogmatic slumber" (acceptance of the rational metaphysics of Christian Wolff), responded to Hume's empirical skepticism with his "Copernican Revolution." Kant effectively synthesized rationalism and empiricism by showing the strengths of each and the weaknesses of each. With rationalists, Kant agreed that the mind is not empty; it possesses categories that are necessary preconditions to organize sensory data. He disagreed with the rationalists' assertion that knowledge begins with ideas. With empiricists, he agreed that knowledge begins with sense experience, but he denied their claim that the mind is empty until it receives sense impressions. Kant utilized a "transcendental argument" to identify the structures of the mind that must be presupposed to have an intelligible experience of the external world.

In addition to Hume's helpful critique of purely rational theistic arguments for God's existence, Hume articulated a devastating critique of miracles. Hume's attack was originally thought definitive and is still embraced by many thinkers today. But Hume's critique had the positive outcome of challenging believers to rethink one of the most frequently used apologetic tools to defend historic Christianity. Anderson (correctly, I believe) shows how Cornelius Van Til's adaptation of Kant's transcendental argument effectively forces people to examine the all-important starting point in any intellectual discussion. Once the naturalistic and materialistic presuppositions of Hume's philosophy are identified, one should not be surprised at his skeptical conclusions. Hume himself expressed that he was confounded by his conclusions, but admitted that he was able only through various diversions to avoid remaining mired in a skeptical mood in his everyday life. Incidentally, some have noted that while C. S. Lewis's apologetic in the majority of his writings was evidentialist in nature, his argument in *Miracles: A Preliminary Study* represents a remarkable change in method. Lewis's tightly argued defense of supernaturalism is one of the finest illustrations of the transcendental method. He effectively demonstrates that supernaturalism, as opposed to Hume's naturalism, not only makes our knowledge of the material world possible but makes the possibility of miracle an open question.

Anderson concludes that Hume's skepticism was believed by many to be a severe detriment to the cause of Christianity. Ironically, his skepticism served the cause of Christian apologetics. While Hume's project proved a failure, Anderson calls it "a highly instructive failure" because it "expose[d] the irrationalism of a naturalistic worldview founded on the autonomy of the human mind." Confronted with such a negative result, those who saw through the skepticism had to begin the epistemological enterprise from exactly the opposite starting point—the transcendent, triune God of Scripture. As sovereign Creator and providential Ruler of his creation, God made humanity in his own image. And he so equipped men and women that they could know themselves, the God who created and ordered the world, and the creation within which they were placed.

The Enlightenment that began so promisingly with Descartes and Bacon in the mid-1600s proved incapable of maintaining its dominance. Just a century and a half later, the Enlightenment era of reason and science was challenged by new prophets, who proposed another radically new worldview. In 1798, William Wordsworth and Samuel Taylor Coleridge published *Lyrical Ballads*. The volume began with "The Rime of the Ancient Mariner" and contained numerous other poetic pieces that worked their way into the English mind as the Romantic movement. Instead of rational and empirical epistemology as autonomous sources of knowledge and rigorous experimental method as the pathway to scientific progress, the Romantics offered still another epistemological starting point. It was just as subjective as Descartes' and Hume's but was distinctively different—human intuition. Rational and scientific order gave way to Romantic wonder, imagination, and feeling. Instead of placing trees in an orderly taxonomy or measuring how many board feet of lumber could be harvested from a tree, Romantics simply proposed encountering the tree in all its beauty.

Romanticism was vaunted in the field of religion on the Continent by Friedrich Schleiermacher, who, a mere year later—1799—penned *Speeches on Religion to Its Cultured Despisers*, aimed at the Romantics in Berlin. The essence of religion lay neither in rational creeds nor in moral choice but in the uniquely human intuitive capacity. For his proposal that religion consisted in *Gefuhl* (the feeling of absolute dependence), Schleiermacher became known as the founder of Protestant liberalism. Anderson underscores how Schleiermacher's liberalism merely furthered the decline of orthodox Christianity that Hume and Kant had initiated.

Thus, the development of Western worldviews continued to unfold. But the contribution of David Hume to that ongoing advancement should not be overlooked. The profound influence of Hume's projects remains foremost in the consciousness of his admirers. Hume reminds believers and skeptics alike that human minds have always sought, continue today, and will seek in the future to understand reality. While exhaustive comprehension of this human quest may lie beyond human grasp, the contemporary reader may start by examining the works of the Great Thinkers series. James Anderson succeeds admirably in meeting the series' threefold goal. *David Hume* is academically informed and addresses Hume's ideas with intellectual integrity; it is epistemically committed to biblical and theological orthodoxy; and it is eminently accessible to informed readers who seek a clear, coherent, and relevant analysis and critique of a salient modern thinker.

W. Andrew Hoffecker
Emeritus Professor of Church History
Reformed Theological Seminary

ACKNOWLEDGMENTS

I wish to thank Catriona Anderson, Johnathon Flippen, and Nathan Shannon for helpful feedback on an earlier version of the manuscript, which prompted me to correct some errors and clarify some obscurities.

INTRODUCTION

WHY HUME MATTERS

Edinburgh's famous Royal Mile runs from the Queen's residence at Holyrood Palace up to Edinburgh Castle. At the corner where the Royal Mile intersects with the Mound, there stands a statue of a seated man. Occasionally seen wearing a traffic cone on his head, courtesy of exuberant and inebriated students, he nevertheless sits in dignified fashion, clothed in a toga and with a book perched on his knee. Every day thousands of people pass by him, but only a small minority of them are aware of the impact that he—or rather, the historical figure he depicts—has had on the culture in which they live and breathe.

Philosophy students at the University of Edinburgh are more aware of his significance, not least because their lectures are held in a building named in his honor: the David Hume Tower. In many ways, Hume is viewed as a heroic figure, not only for the School of Philosophy, but also for the university as a whole—both the humanities and the sciences—representing, as he does, the legacy of the Scottish Enlightenment. Hume's significance was confirmed by a poll conducted by the *Sunday Times* in 1999, which awarded him the title "Greatest Scot of the

Millennium," edging out his close friend, the economist Adam Smith.

Hume's impact on Western civilization can scarcely be overstated. Traces of his thought can be detected in almost every aspect of our culture today. It was Hume's writings that famously roused Immanuel Kant from his "dogmatic slumber" and motivated his "Copernican revolution," which in large measure set the epistemological agenda for the next two centuries. It would hardly be an exaggeration to say that without Hume, there would have been no Kant; and without Kant, no Hegel; and without Hegel, no Marx. Friedrich Schleiermacher, the pioneer of Protestant liberalism, propounded his new understanding of Christianity as grounded in religious experience, rather than verbal divine revelation, in response to the critiques put forward by Hume and Kant. Hume's influential objections to natural theology (arguments for the existence and attributes of God based on natural reason) and to claims of miracles (such as the apostolic testimony to the resurrection of Jesus) may have been more responsible for the subsequent decline of orthodox Christianity in the English-speaking world than anything else. One often encounters today the received wisdom that revealed religion has never recovered from the "double hammer blow" of Hume and Kant.

Hume's empiricist epistemology provided the inspiration for the logical positivist movement in the early twentieth century, according to which metaphysical, moral, and theological claims are cognitively meaningless: they don't even rise to the level of falsehood. Logical positivism quickly succumbed to its own internal contradictions, but its spirit lives on in the crude scientism of the New Atheists and other modern critics of supernaturalism.

Hume's innovative moral theory was arguably the primary influence on the utilitarianism of Jeremy Bentham and John

Stuart Mill, a theory that underwrites many secular approaches to ethics today. Hume is certainly the patron saint of philosophers who seek a wholly naturalistic grounding for moral norms.

Meanwhile, in the philosophy of science, Hume's ghost continues to loom over theories of causation and the laws of nature. The so-called problem of induction, the classic formulation of which is credited to Hume, remains a central problem in the philosophy of science, for which no widely accepted solution exists. Were it not for Hume's critical analysis of inductive inference, Karl Popper would not have proposed his influential falsifiability criterion for scientific theories.

The above is but a sampling of the areas and disciplines in which Hume's impact continues to be felt. Although he addresses a wide range of disparate topics, his writings have an underlying unity and consistency insofar as they represent the outworking of an ambitious philosophical and scientific program to understand the world, especially human thought and action, in entirely naturalistic terms. In a real sense, the credibility of Christianity hangs on the cogency of Hume's critique of supernaturalism. For that reason alone, Hume's thought demands our attention and assessment.

The goal of this book is therefore twofold: (1) to provide a summary exposition of the major points of Hume's thought, and (2) to offer a critical assessment of them from a distinctively Reformed perspective. In the process, I hope to show that Hume's arguments, far from refuting the Christian worldview, indirectly support that worldview by exposing the self-defeating implications of naturalism.

ABBREVIATIONS

DNR	*Dialogues concerning Natural Religion*
EHU	*An Enquiry concerning Human Understanding*
EPM	*An Enquiry concerning the Principles of Morals*
NHR	*The Natural History of Religion* (as found in *Four Dissertations*)
THN	*A Treatise of Human Nature*

The works are cited by book (where applicable), part, section, and paragraph, in that order. For example, *THN* 1.2.3.4 refers to book 1, part 2, section 3, paragraph 4 of *A Treatise of Human Nature*, and *DNR* 1.2 refers to part 1, paragraph 2 of *Dialogues concerning Natural Religion*.

1

HUME'S LIFE AND WORKS

David Hume was born in Edinburgh on April 26, 1711, the second of two sons of Joseph Home. (As an aspiring author, Hume later modified the spelling of his surname to make its pronunciation more self-evident.) Hume's father died shortly after his son's second birthday, and the boy was raised single-handedly by his mother, whom he described fondly as "a woman of singular merit." His early childhood was spent at the family home in Ninewells, located in the Scottish Borders some fifty miles from Edinburgh. Hume's mother found him to be an unusually gifted child, so when his brother John left home for university studies in Edinburgh at fourteen (the usual age at that time), David accompanied him, despite being several years younger.

At the university, Hume received a well-rounded education that included competence in the classical languages, history, literature, metaphysics, ethics, logic, mathematics, and elements of the natural sciences. After leaving Edinburgh, he embarked on a career in law, as his family had encouraged him to do, but Hume had scant enthusiasm for it and found himself far more energized by reading works of classical literature and philosophy. As he later recounted, "I found an insurmountable aversion to every-thing but the pursuits of philosophy and general learning; and while they fancied that I was reading Voet and Vinnius, Cicero and Virgil were the authors I was secretly devouring." From an early age, Hume aspired to the life of "a man of letters," reading widely and addressing himself in manifold writings to the press-ing topics of the day.

At some point during this period of personal studies at the family home in Ninewells, Hume apparently experienced a light-bulb moment, as a result of which he resolved to devote all his powers of examination to what he cryptically described as "a new Scene of Thought." This intense intellectual project apparently took a toll on his health, both physical and mental, requiring a physician's prescription of medication and exercise. Hume's family was not wealthy, and he realized that he would need to find gainful employment, so he took a position in a merchant's business in Bristol with the hope that it would improve his con-dition with a "more active Scene of Life." But the venture was short-lived. In 1734, Hume decided to relocate to rural France, where he could live more economically while devoting himself wholeheartedly to his philosophical interests.

Thus it was in France that Hume, at the young age of 23, embarked upon his first and most ambitious philosophical work, *A Treatise of Human Nature.* The central goal of this three-volume treatise was to develop a "science of human nature." Put simply, Hume aspired to do for human nature what he believed Isaac Newton and other "natural philosophers" had done for the realm outside of human affairs: to develop a rigorously *naturalistic* account of human thought and action, particularly our moral and aesthetic judgments, which would rely exclusively upon *empir-ical* investigation. One major feature of this work would be its examination of our intellectual faculties and an exploration of the capacity—and, in some important respects, the incapacity—

of human reason to deliver genuine knowledge of ourselves and the world we inhabit.

Hume returned to England in 1737 to prepare the work for publication. Books 1 and 2 ("Of the Understanding" and "Of the Passions") were published anonymously in 1739.[1] Book 3, "Of Morals," which built on the foundational principles laid down in the first two volumes, appeared the following year, together with an "Abstract" that summarized his major theses and addressed some misunderstandings and objections raised by early reviewers.

In a reflection on his intellectual career, written toward the end of his life, Hume famously remarked that the *Treatise* "fell deadborn from the press." This was an exaggeration. The work did not establish Hume's reputation, as he had hoped, but it garnered plenty of attention, much of it highly critical, even though he had opted at the eleventh hour to remove some material that would have been viewed as a direct assault on religion. Nevertheless, the *Treatise* offered more than enough to fuel concerns that its author was an infidel propounding a dangerous skepticism that would tend to undermine public morals. As a consequence, Hume never held an academic position in his life, despite being nominated for one at Edinburgh and another at Glasgow. The critics who campaigned against his appointments prevailed over his supporters.

The year 1741 saw the publication of the first volume of Hume's *Essays, Moral and Political,* in which he addressed himself to various philosophical and historical debates of the time. His critical musings gained him further admirers, and a second volume appeared the following year.

After a brief, unhappy spell as a private tutor, followed by

---

1. The anonymity was due partly to the controversial content of some portions of the *Treatise,* although it was not uncommon at that time for new authors to publish anonymously.

a more satisfying secretarial role on a European diplomatic mission, Hume published *An Enquiry concerning Human Understanding* (1748). This was essentially a more streamlined reworking of book 1 of the *Treatise*, along with some material from book 2. Of particular note was the addition of Hume's provocative argument against miracles, which he had decided to excise from the *Treatise*. This first *Enquiry* was followed three years later by a "recasting" of book 3 of the *Treatise* under the title *An Enquiry concerning the Principles of Morals*. "Of all my writings," Hume would later declare, the second *Enquiry* was "incomparably the best."

The relationship between the *Treatise* and the two *Enquiries*, and the extent to which Hume changed his views, are matters of ongoing debate among Hume scholars. Some of his earlier arguments were refined, others were dropped altogether, and a number of new arguments were introduced. Overall the differences are more matters of style and rhetorical strategy than matters of substance. How Hume himself viewed the *Enquiries* is open to interpretation. He referred later to the *Treatise* as a "juvenile work" that he had sent to press "too early." He invited his readers to treat the *Enquiries* as the definitive, mature statement of his views, containing answers to his earlier critics. While the aim of the *Enquiries* was to "cast the whole anew," he insisted that the "philosophical principles are the same" as in the *Treatise*. Hume averred that the main shortcomings of the latter lay in the presentation, not the substance. For this reason, scholars typically draw from both sets of works when expounding and evaluating Hume's philosophy (a policy to be followed in this book).

In the 1750s, Hume produced further collections of essays on a wide range of topics, including literature, history, ethics, and politics. His appointment as the librarian of the Faculty of Advocates in Edinburgh afforded him both time and opportunity to work on his magisterial six-volume *History of England*

(1754–62). Although it was far from apolitical—Hume's opinions are never hidden from the reader and are often pithily expressed—Hume prided himself on having adopted the stance of a more objective historian, relative to his predecessors, at least. On some points, Hume appeared to side with the Tory reading of events, on others with the Whigs. Hume's political inclinations were mainly conservative and royalist; the *History* presented a more sympathetic view of the Stuart monarchs and was correspondingly scathing about the Cromwellian interregnum. Whatever the virtues and vices of Hume's historical works, they enjoyed great commercial success, being reprinted several times with extensive revisions by Hume in response to critical reviews. Royalties from the series provided Hume with financial stability and modest comfort for the rest of his life.

During the same period, Hume published four major dissertations, the first of which, "The Natural History of Religion," presented a nonsupernaturalist account of the development of religion. He attempted to explain the origins of religion on the basis of his account of human nature, coupled with an evolutionary psychology in which the passions of hope and especially fear serve as driving forces. According to Hume, the earliest form of religion was a crude polytheism, which was later refined into monotheism, although the latter inevitably tends to relapse into polytheistic elements. In this work, Hume deliberately sidestepped the question of whether religious beliefs could claim any rational or empirical support. The essay was pitched as a genealogical reconstruction, rather than an epistemological critique.

Hume spent the years 1763–65 serving at the British Embassy in Paris. It was during this second sojourn in France that the Scotsman encountered the controversial writer Jean-Jacques Rousseau (1712–78). Despite the significant differences between their political philosophies, they formed a bond of friendship, and later on Hume provided a safe haven in London when Rousseau's position in Switzerland became precarious. Within a year, however, the friendship degenerated, largely due to Rousseau's erratic and paranoid behavior, and it eventually collapsed into a bitter breach with recriminations on both sides.

After some further years of political service, Hume retired to Edinburgh in 1769, where he lived out his remaining years in the company of friends and spent his time mainly on revising his earlier works and composing responses to his critics. One of the reworked pieces was his now-famous *Dialogues concerning Natural Religion*, in which three fictional characters debate whether natural theology—in particular, the argument from design—can furnish any reliable knowledge of the divine attributes. Although the original draft had been penned many years earlier, even after revision Hume judged it too incendiary to be published in his lifetime.

By 1772, Hume's health had begun to fail, and three years later he was diagnosed with intestinal cancer. Given his notoriously irreligious views, his critics wondered whether the prospect of imminent death would elicit something of a recantation. They were to be disappointed. His close friends, such as the economist Adam Smith, testified that Hume approached his end with serenity, magnanimity, and irreverent humor, finding satisfaction in his accomplishments and confidence in the fact (as he saw it) that while there was no evidence for a heavenly afterlife, neither was there any reason to fear a hellish one. A skeptic to the last, Hume died on August 25, 1776, leaving directions that he should be buried at his own expense under a monument on Edinburgh's Calton Hill, overlooking the city he considered his home. Among his other instructions was the request that his nephew arrange for the publication of his *Dialogues concerning Natural Religion*, which duly hit the presses in 1779 and sealed Hume's reputation as one of the most formidable critics of religion in Christendom.

2

HUME'S PHILOSOPHICAL PROJECT

Hume's central focus and aim in his philosophical writings are not hard to discern. His subject matter, as the title of his *Treatise* indicates, is "human nature"—specifically, our intellectual, moral, and aesthetic faculties—and the subtitle reveals what he seeks to accomplish: "an attempt to introduce the experimental method of reasoning into moral subjects." By "moral subjects," Hume means not merely what we would normally describe as ethics (although that is a central concern), but the entire realm of human experience, judgment, and action. This he proposes to investigate by "the experimental method of reasoning," relying solely upon empirical observations and what can be reliably inferred from them.

Why did Hume devote himself to this project? Like many in his day, Hume was impressed with developments in the natural sciences pioneered by such thinkers as Isaac Newton (1642–1727). Besides advancements in mathematics, great progress had been made in identifying laws of nature that enabled reliable predictions to be made about events in the natural world, such as the future locations of planets and other heavenly bodies. The discipline of philosophy was in disarray, scandalized by seemingly irresolvable disagreements about the nature of God, the nature of the soul, the basic constitution of the universe, and the foundations of ethics. In stark contrast, so it seemed, the discipline of science was delivering genuine progress. Hume attributed this success to a strict use of the "experimental method," setting aside speculations and hypotheses based on abstract reasonings that were not anchored in observable facts.

Hume recognized, however, that the natural sciences are human endeavors. They are the product of human observations and inferences, and thus "all the sciences have a relation, greater or less, to human nature" and are "in some measure dependent on the science of MAN" (*THN* Intro.4). Since no building can be more stable than its foundations, it was imperative for him to develop a *science of human nature* that is investigated and expounded no less rigorously than the sciences that are dependent upon it. Just as there are laws governing the motions of physical objects, so must there be laws governing human thoughts and actions, but in Hume's view the latter had not received nearly enough attention and critical scrutiny. Indeed, Hume was concerned that the powers of the human intellectual faculties had been in some respects wildly overestimated. An audit was long overdue.

Hume therefore set himself the task of explaining "the principles of human nature" and thereby opening the door to "a complete system of the sciences, built on a foundation almost entirely new, and the only one upon which they can stand with any security" (*THN* Intro.6). In short, Hume aspired to apply the scientific method to human nature, just as Newton had applied it to the rest of nature, and in so doing to develop an integrated scientific worldview encompassing everything from the hydrological cycle to the casting of ballots in voting booths.

Three Distinctives of the Project

The distinctives of Hume's philosophical project can be summarized in three words: *empiricism, naturalism,* and *skepticism.*

Empiricism. Hume vows in his introduction to the *Treatise* that the science of human nature must rigorously apply the "experimental method" in the same manner as the natural sciences, by which he means reliance on empirical observations alone:

> As the science of man is the only solid foundation for the other sciences, so the only solid foundation we can give to this science itself must be laid on *experience and observation.* (*THN* Intro.7, emphasis added)

> For to me it seems evident, that the essence of the mind being equally unknown to us with that of external bodies, it must be equally impossible to form any notion of its powers and qualities *otherwise than from careful and exact experiments,* and the observation of those particular effects, which result from its different circumstances and situations. And tho' we must endeavour to render all our principles as universal as possible, by tracing up our experiments to the utmost, and explaining all effects from the simplest and fewest causes, 'tis still certain *we cannot go beyond experience*; and any hypothesis, that pretends to discover the ultimate original qualities of human nature, ought at first to be rejected as presumptuous and chimerical. (*THN* Intro.8, emphasis added)

> None of [the sciences] can go beyond experience, or establish any principles which are not founded on that authority. (*THN* Intro.10)

Hume's conclusions are thus to be drawn from careful reflection on his own nature (both his experiences of the world and his inner thoughts and feelings) and from "a cautious observation of human life" more generally. This thoroughgoing empiricism doesn't exclude the use of reason, but it does mean that reason cannot serve as a source of knowledge apart from experience. Hume rules out any appeal to *a priori* principles, other than purely logical truths. Innate knowledge—if there be such a thing—is off the table.

Naturalism. Hume's project is also thoroughly naturalistic in the sense that it aspires to be thoroughly scientific, appealing only to data delivered by experience and explaining phenomena solely in terms of law-like principles of cause and effect. Hume's operating assumption is that humans are no less a part of the natural order than rocks, plants, and (other) animals. The same mechanistic picture of the natural world represented by Newtonian physics must be applied to the world of human affairs. In significant respects, Hume anticipated the Darwinian evolutionary view of man's place in the world.[1]

Among other things, this precludes any appeal to supernatural sources or causes: angels, spirits, immaterial souls, or God. It is important to note that for Hume this is a *methodological,* rather than a *metaphysical,* naturalism. He doesn't mean to adopt a dogmatic *a priori* stance with respect to the ultimate nature of reality (although, one might argue, the result is much the same). As we will see later, Hume's skepticism undercuts any such metaphysical dogmatism. He doesn't rule out *a priori* the existence of God, nor does he rule it in. He merely insists that a proper science of human nature must refer only to natural explanations. In the end, this is just a methodological consequence of Hume's empiricism.

1. "He was a Darwinian before his time, an apostle, if anything, of evolved human nature and human sentiment" (Simon Blackburn, *How to Read Hume* [London: Granta Books, 2008], 13).

Skepticism. Hume is commonly described as a skeptic, a label that became attached to him in his own lifetime. Indeed, in his own writings he candidly characterizes his philosophy as a skeptical one. It is not, however, a radical skepticism that invites us to abandon our commonsense beliefs about ourselves and the world. Hume explicitly disavows a "Pyrrhonean skepticism," according to which we should withhold judgment on all matters. On the contrary, Hume holds that we *cannot* adopt such a position; it is constitutionally impossible for us not to believe those things we normally take for granted.

What Hume advocates instead is a mitigated skepticism directed toward human reason. Put bluntly, Hume thinks that reason is overrated and that we must recognize its limitations. Philosophers have labored to establish various momentous theses by the power of reason—moral principles, metaphysical axioms, religious doctrines—but reason is inherently incapable of delivering the goods. Such claims must be founded on experience, with reason in a merely supporting role, or else we must concede that they lack rational justification. This doesn't mean that we must jettison those beliefs—at least, not all of them. It does entail, however, that we must find another explanation for why we hold them. Hume's science of human nature doesn't so much seek to justify our beliefs as to explain the processes by which we acquire them. At root, it is a *descriptive* project, rather than a *defensive* one.

A Two-Phase Project

Broadly speaking, Hume's proposed science of human nature proceeds in two phases: the first *critical* and the second *constructive*. The goal of the critical phase, as indicated above, is to demonstrate the limits of human reason. Whatever the topic under examination, Hume seeks to show that no useful conclusions can be derived from reason alone. Thus, to give some prominent examples, Hume contends that reason by itself (1) cannot ground any moral principles, (2) cannot motivate us to any actions, (3) cannot justify our beliefs about causal relationships, (4) cannot vindicate any metaphysical theories, and (5) cannot prove the existence of God. In so doing, Hume is deliberately taking aim at earlier philosophers, such as G. W. Leibniz and John Locke, as well as many of his contemporaries.

While this critical phase has received the lion's share of attention and analysis, it would be quite unfair to characterize Hume's project as predominantly negative and skeptical, for it also has a positive aspect that is no less interesting. In fact, the bulk of the *Treatise* and the two *Enquiries* is devoted to this constructive phase. The critical phase merely clears the ground for Hume's new science of man, which offers an account of human nature on the firm foundation of empirical observation. Some of the demolished edifices, such as theological metaphysics, are lost causes and shouldn't be mourned. Yet other areas of human interest, such as moral principles, aesthetic judgments, and scientific investigation, Hume proposes to explain in terms of his "scientific" account of the human mind, to which we now turn.

Hume's Theory of the Mind

Hume's account of the human mind begins with what he calls *perceptions,* a catch-all category for all mental phenomena: concepts, thoughts, beliefs, feelings, motivations, and so forth. Perceptions may be propositional (e.g., a judgment about some factual claim) or non-propositional (e.g., the sensation one experiences when touching a hot surface). In Hume's day, it was generally assumed that we don't perceive things directly; instead, our knowledge of the world is mediated by our perceptions. On this view, the human mind can be likened to a theater screen on which images appear that represent the world. When I see and hear a cow, strictly speaking, I'm not perceiving the cow directly (as though the cow itself were in immediate contact with my mind); rather, I'm experiencing representative perceptions, which I take to be caused, via my sensory organs, by a cow. This "theory of ideas" was largely taken for granted because there can be *perceptions of things* without there being *things perceived*. For example, we can "see" cows in our dreams and can suffer from hallucinations.

Hume proposes that perceptions be divided into *impressions* and *ideas*. Although he speaks of these as "two distinct kinds" of perceptions, it turns out that the difference is really one of degree, not of kind. Impressions are characterized by the "force and vivacity" with which they strike the mind. They are generally what we would consider primary or immediate experiences: the taste of fresh coffee, the warm sensation as it flows over your tongue, the happiness you feel as you drink it, and the overwhelming desire to accompany it with a doughnut.

Ideas, on the other hand, are merely "faint images of these in thinking and reasoning." Hence, your later recollection of drinking the coffee is an idea rather than an impression. It is a real experience, but far less "lively" than the original experience. Hume assumes that everyone will grant the distinction between impressions and ideas insofar as they recognize a difference between *feeling* and *thinking*.

Hume further distinguishes between external and internal impressions: *impressions of sensation*, such as the warmth of the coffee, and *impressions of reflection*, which are formed in response to ideas. Thus, for example, if your recollection of the coffee prompts a desire to buy another one, then that desire would be a *reflection*: a "secondary" (internal) rather than "original" (external) impression.

Impressions and ideas may be *simple* or *complex*. Consider the experience of eating a tomato. You have simple impressions of the redness, roundness, and sweetness of the tomato, but these may be combined into the complex impression of the tomato as a whole. Conversely, when you later bring to mind the complex idea of the tomato, you can distinguish the simple idea of its redness from that of its sweetness. This distinction allows Hume to account for the fact that we can have ideas about things we have never actually observed: for instance, we can combine the idea of a horse with the idea of a horn (both of which we derive from experience) into the idea of a unicorn, despite not having observed such a creature.

Having drawn these various distinctions, Hume introduces a "general proposition" that amounts to a "first principle" in his science of human nature:

> All our simple ideas in their first appearance are deriv'd from simple impressions, which are correspondent to them, and which they exactly represent. (THN 1.1.1.7, emphasis original)

This thesis, generally known as the Copy Principle, serves as a lynchpin in Hume's empiricism. Every simple *idea* is a derivative copy of a simple *impression*, and thus must be traceable back to that original impression. Hume offers two basic arguments in support of the Copy Principle. The first draws on his own experiences, with the implication that anyone can replicate them: whenever he reflects on the origin of an idea, he can see that it corresponds to an earlier impression, and since the latter precedes the former in time, the former must derive from the latter. The second argument amounts to a challenge to the reader to produce an example of a simple idea that is not derived from a simple impression. Hume is confident that no such counterexample can be produced—or at least, if one can, it amounts to an exception that confirms the rule.

The Copy Principle, it turns out, has a correlative that allows one to distinguish meaningful from meaningless mental content. If a philosopher (or indeed anyone) makes use of an idea that cannot be derived from simple impressions, that idea is cognitively vacuous and thus should be set aside. Any term that purports to refer to such an idea is strictly undefinable. As we will see, this correlative principle is a sword that Hume will wield repeatedly in support of his skeptical conclusions.

Hume also has something to say about the various *faculties* of the mind that produce and process our various perceptions. There are faculties that generate the impressions of sensation and reflection (although Hume has little to say about these other than to assume them). There are also two basic faculties that produce our ideas: *memory* and *imagination*. *Memory* is straightforward enough: it is the faculty that brings forth an idea representing an earlier impression (e.g., of the coffee). *Imagination* is more versatile, however, because it can disassemble complex ideas, construct new ones (e.g., the idea of a unicorn), and lead us by various "principles of association" from one idea to another. Hume maintains that he can reduce these associative principles to three: *resemblance, contiguity,* and *cause and effect.* As an example, consider a series of photographs of a mountain. By *resemblance,* the idea of a photograph of the mountain leads to the idea of the mountain itself. By *contiguity,* the idea of one photograph leads to the idea of the next photograph. By *cause and effect,* the idea of the photographs leads to the idea of the camera that produced them.

The trouble with the faculty of imagination, however, is that its ideas aren't always well founded. Some are the products of *reason* (which Hume typically calls "the understanding"), while others are products of mere *fancy.* Hume argues that reason can only establish two types of conclusion: *relations of ideas* and *matters of fact.* Examples of the first type would be mathematical relationships (e.g., the Pythagorean theorem) and definitional truths (e.g., that all bachelors are unmarried). This type of reasoning

Hume refers to as "abstract" because it concerns only the relationships between ideas, not between our ideas and factual matters in the world. It is deductive in nature and its conclusions enjoy logical certainty. Reasoning about matters of fact, on the other hand, is only probabilistic, because one can always draw false conclusions. For example, based on your earlier observation of a silver Mercedes in the parking lot, you might reason that you are now observing the very same vehicle in that location. Or, drawing on your many observations of wet ground after rain, you might reason from the wetness of the ground (an impression) that it has recently rained. Such beliefs would be justified, yet could still be mistaken.

This bifurcation of reasonable beliefs into *relations of ideas* and *matters of fact* has been dubbed *Hume's Fork*, and its author applies it to various topics with frequently skeptical conclusions. Hume contends that a large proportion of our natural beliefs—matters of common sense, we might say—cannot be justified by reason, all of which underscores the woeful limitations of reason. Consider some of the beliefs that you likely take for granted:

- That an external world exists independently of your experiences of it.
- That every event must have a cause.
- That future events will resemble past ones.
- That there is such a thing as a "self," which is the subject of your experiences.
- That you have (or are) an immaterial soul that will survive the death of your body.
- That the world is guided by a benevolent providence.

None of these beliefs, Hume suggests, can be rationally justified, even though it might be psychologically difficult (or even impossible) for us to relinquish them.

A New Account of Causation

One philosophical issue to which Hume most notoriously applied his skeptical analysis is that of *causation*. In fact, in the "Abstract" of the *Treatise*, Hume remarked that his discussion of causation constituted the "chief argument" of his magnum opus. Hume fully appreciated the central role that causal reasoning plays in our understanding of the world, from scientific investigation and cutting-edge engineering to the simplest of actions, such as turning a key in a lock. But what is causation? And how does causal reasoning actually work?

For the medieval scholars, Aristotle's analysis of causation provided the standard account. Following the Renaissance and the waning of scholastic philosophy, a more mechanistic view of causation came to prevail. The prevailing view was that the world is filled with substances (individual things) that possess causal powers to bring about changes in other substances. Thus, when the bat hits the ball, the event of the ball flying into the air necessarily follows the event of the bat connecting with the ball, because of some intrinsic power or force within the bat.

Hume is profoundly dissatisfied with this viewpoint. In the first place, he argues on the basis of his empiricist theory of ideas that we can have no meaningful idea of a causal power. We certainly have an impression of one event (the bat connecting with the ball) and an impression of a succeeding event (the ball flying into the air). What we emphatically do not possess, however, is any impression of a mysterious power or force that connects the two events. A true science of human nature requires a more scientific account of causation, and Hume gives it his best shot.

According to Hume's analysis, causation is a complex idea composed of three simple ideas: *temporal priority* (a cause must precede its effect), *spatial proximity* (a cause must be near its effect), and *necessary connection* (an effect follows from its cause by necessity). The last of these is the problematic one. Traditionally the notion of necessary connection was explained in terms of intrinsic causal powers, but Hume denies even the intelligibility of such an idea. Furthermore, the notion of a necessary connection cannot be defended on a consistently empiricist basis. We may observe that the ball flies into the air when the bat hits it, but we don't observe any necessity about it. No matter how many times we observe those conjoined events, it wouldn't follow that the one event *must* follow the other. It is logically possible for the ball not to behave that way on some future occasion.[2] In fact, the very concept of necessity is problematic, given Hume's empiricism. Our impressions can only convey to us what *does* happen; they cannot tell us what *must* happen.[3]

Such is the deconstructive phase of Hume's treatment of causation. What then is his constructive alternative? Hume doesn't want to abandon altogether the idea of necessary connection because he knows it is essential to our idea of causation. What he offers instead is a new account of how we acquire that idea, an account that appeals to habituation rather than reason. The first stage in the account involves our observation of a *constant conjunction* of similar events. For example, every time we observe a bat connecting with a ball, we immediately observe the ball flying into the air. These two kinds of events—bat-hitting and ball-flying—are invariably conjoined. Over time, we become psychologically habituated to this conjunction, such that whenever we observe the first type of event, we naturally expect the second type of event to follow (*EHU* 5.1.5–8).[4] This sense of

2. For Hume, anything that can be conceived without logical contradiction is possible. See, e.g., *THN* 1.2.2.8, 1.3.3.3, 1.3.6.5; *EHU* 4.2, 4.18, 5.11.

3. Hume is thinking here in terms of physical or natural necessity (i.e., the kind of necessity associated with laws of nature), as opposed to logical necessity.

4. By way of analogy, think of Pavlov's dogs, which were conditioned to salivate upon hearing the sound of a bell.

expectation that we experience is a secondary impression from which we derive our idea of necessary connection. Since we have a natural tendency to ascribe secondary qualities to objects themselves (e.g., we treat the blueness of the sky as if it were an objective feature of the sky itself, rather than a subjective feature of our impressions of the sky), we treat this causal necessity as though it were an objective, intrinsic feature of the world (*EHU* 7.2.28–29). Such a belief is perfectly natural, in Hume's view, even though it isn't rationally justified.

Hume's account of causation is radically revisionist. Causation turns out to be a psychological feature of our minds, rather than a metaphysical feature of the world. Hume doesn't rule out the existence of the latter; he simply insists that we take a skeptical position, withholding judgment. Even if there *are* real causal powers operative in the world, we cannot know anything about them, and they cannot be the source of our idea of causation.

Philosophy Psychologized

Philosophy has been traditionally divided into three major fields: metaphysics, epistemology, and ethics. Hume's project leads him to depart radically from the received views in all three areas. As to metaphysics, he is a thoroughgoing skeptic. Our minds are simply not equipped to prove or disprove speculative theories about substances, causal powers, the existence and persistence of the soul, the origins of the cosmos, and the existence of a mind-independent world. This skepticism is expressed most famously in the closing paragraph of the first *Enquiry*:

> When we run over libraries, persuaded of these principles, what havoc must we make? If we take in our hand any volume; of divinity or school metaphysics, for instance; let us ask, *Does it contain any abstract reasoning concerning quantity or number?*

No. *Does it contain any experimental reasoning concerning matter of fact and existence?* No. Commit it then to the flames: For it can contain nothing but sophistry and illusion. (*EHU* 12.3.34)

Hume's position is crystal clear: metaphysics, in its traditional guise, is dead on arrival.

What about epistemology? Traditionally, epistemologists have been concerned with normative questions about our beliefs and how they are grounded. What is knowledge, and what distinguishes it from beliefs that just happen to be true? What counts as a justified belief? In the most general terms, what distinguishes good beliefs from bad ones?

Rather surprisingly, Hume doesn't directly address such normative questions, and they don't feature as a central concern for him. Hume's project is focused primarily on factual questions regarding how we form our beliefs and why we believe what we do. In short, Hume is engaged in psychology, rather than epistemology; he offers a descriptive account of human thought, rather than a prescriptive one. This makes sense if we recall that his goal is a scientific account of human nature, for science is concerned with how things do in fact go, rather than how things ought to go.

Insofar as Hume speaks to more traditional epistemological questions, his general assumption is that knowledge is acquired only through the faculty of the understanding (i.e., reason). This faculty offers two modes of reasoning, corresponding to the two prongs of Hume's Fork: *demonstrative* reasoning about relations of ideas (e.g., mathematical deductions) and *probabilistic* reasoning about matters of fact (e.g., the inference that the sun will rise tomorrow since it has been observed to rise every previous day). The latter mode of reasoning is fallible and cannot deliver deductive certainty. Hume treats beliefs formed by either of these modes as epistemically respectable. As we will consider later, however, he raises a serious problem for probabilistic reasoning, which brings its rational basis into grave doubt. In addition, Hume raises critical questions about the very idea of an objective, mind-independent world lying behind our impressions. In the end, Hume's epistemology—insofar as he develops one—is exceedingly modest. We can know the internal relations between our ideas, and our immediate impressions of a spatio-temporal world, and that's about it.

In the name of science, then, Hume banishes metaphysics and psychologizes epistemology. In the next chapter, we will see how, on much the same basis, he also psychologizes ethics.

3

HUME'S NATURALISTIC ETHICS

At the turn of the eighteenth century, Europe still considered itself Christian, even while orthodox Christian teachings were being challenged in various quarters of the church and the academy. One of the questions provoking much debate in Hume's day concerned the foundations of ethics. The mainstream view was that moral laws originated with God: they are essentially divine commands, received through natural and special revelation (specifically, the conscience and the teachings of Scripture). In the early Enlightenment period, however, this traditional position was found wanting. Even if moral laws were received through divine revelation, they would still require some justification on the basis of human reason and experience, so it was argued.

Three theories about morality dominated the field. First, there were *self-interest theories*, defended by such thinkers as Thomas Hobbes (1588–1679) and Bernard Mandeville (1670–1733), who argued that moral convictions arise out of our natural tendency toward self-love and self-preservation. We keep our promises, pay our taxes, and care for our neighbors because such actions serve our own ends, and that explains why we regard them as "good." On such a view, there are no God-ordained "natural" laws. Rules of morality exist only out of practical necessity, a social compromise designed to restrain our selfish instincts and impose some degree of civilization. Needless to say, these theories were regarded as shocking in their day and provoked a broader debate over the foundations of morality.

One significant response to self-interest theories was provided by the *moral rationalists*. The rationalists maintained that moral principles, which are universal and necessary, can be derived from reason alone. On this view, moral truths are analogous to mathematical truths. Samuel Clarke's (1675–1729) moral theory hinged on the idea that there are necessary relations between persons—not only between fellow men, but supremely between man and God—and from these relations moral principles can be deduced in much the same way that mathematical principles can be deduced from relations between numbers. This theory had the advantage of promising deductive certainty about moral laws, at least in principle. Insofar as our motivation to act morally is grounded in reasons for our actions, immorality amounts to irrationality.

The other major alternative was offered by the *moral sense theorists*, among whom the 3rd Earl of Shaftsbury (1671–1713) and Francis Hutcheson (1694–1746) were considered leading lights. This approach was far more empiricist in orientation, positing that we possess a basic moral sense that allows us to perceive moral qualities in people and their actions, in a manner analogous to other forms of sense perception such as vision. This moral sense was typically assumed to be a God-given natural faculty.

In this three-way debate, Hume sided with the moral sense theorists, defending a version of moral sentimentalism that accords with his overall philosophical project. We will proceed by reviewing his critiques of rationalist and self-interest theories before considering his own constructive proposal.

Against Moral Rationalism

Hume's main target in the *Treatise* is Clarke's moral rationalism. His critique can be boiled down to two lines of objection: (1) Our moral judgments must have the power to motivate us toward action, but reason as such has no power to do so. (2) Our faculty of reason ("the understanding") can only establish truths about relations of ideas or matters of fact, but neither can ground moral principles.

Regarding the first objection, Hume observes that rationalists see the moral life as a struggle to bring the passions under the rule of reason. Both motivate our actions, they say, but reason alone moves us toward moral actions, often in opposition to our passions (that is, our affections and desires). To the contrary, Hume argues, while reason can tell us what is true or false about the world in which we live, that alone provides no motivation whatsoever to act one way or the other, nor could it overcome any passion. Passions are neither true nor false, which means there could never be a conflict between a motivation to act and a deliverance of reason. To regard a motivation as unreasonable as such is to commit a category mistake. Hume makes his point in the most startling fashion:

> 'Tis not contrary to reason to prefer the destruction of the whole world to the scratching of my finger. 'Tis not contrary to reason for me to chuse [*sic*] my total ruin, to prevent the least uneasiness of an Indian or person wholly unknown to me. 'Tis as little contrary to reason to prefer even my own acknowledg'd lesser good to my greater, and have a more ardent affection for the former than the latter. (*THN* 2.3.3.6)

It is important to note that Hume does not deny that reason plays a role in moral action. His only point is that reason alone cannot move the will. The passions play the lead part, while reason plays a merely supporting role: "Reason is, and ought to be only the slave of the passions, and can never pretend to any other office than to serve and obey them" (*THN* 2.3.3.4).

Hume's second objection to moral rationalism is that reason by itself cannot deliver any moral knowledge. Hume's Fork is again brought to bear on the question:

> If the thought and understanding were alone capable of fixing the boundaries of right and wrong, the character of virtuous and vicious either must lie in some *relations of objects*, or must be a *matter of fact*, which is discovered by our reasoning. This consequence is evident. As the operations of human understanding divide themselves into two kinds, the comparing of ideas, and the inferring of matter of fact; were virtue discover'd by the understanding; it must be an object of one of these operations. (*THN* 3.1.1.18, emphasis added)

On the one hand, moral truths cannot be reduced to "relations of objects," because two pairs of objects can stand in the same relation even though only one of the pairings is associated with immorality. Hume offers the example of parricide: when a man kills his parent, we may judge it immoral, but when a sapling grows up and overcomes the oak tree that produced it, we never judge it immoral. In both cases, the progeny destroys the progenitor, yet that relationship alone doesn't entail any moral conclusion.

As for the second prong of the Fork, Hume invites us to reflect on any immoral action, such as a case of willful murder, and consider whether any observed facts about the object of our reflection entail its immorality. Hume is confident that no "vice" can be found in mere matters of fact, whether singly or jointly. The argument culminates in his famous observation about a common error in moral reasoning (the so-called "is-ought fallacy"):

> In every system of morality, which I have hitherto met with, I have always remark'd, that the author proceeds for some time in the ordinary way of reasoning, and establishes the being of a God, or makes observations concerning human affairs; when of a sudden I am surpriz'd to find, that instead of the usual copulations of propositions, *is*, and *is not*, I meet with no proposition that is not connected with an *ought*, or an *ought not*. This change is imperceptible; but is, however, of the last consequence. For as this *ought*, or *ought not*, expresses some new relation or affirmation, 'tis necessary that it shou'd be observ'd and explain'd; and at the same time that a reason should be given, for what seems altogether inconceivable, how this new relation can be a deduction from others, which are entirely different from it. (*THN* 3.1.1.27)

In sum, the fatal flaw in moral rationalism is that the faculty of understanding can tell us only what *is* or *is not*; it is powerless to tell us what *ought* or *ought not* to be.

These antirationalist arguments serve as staging for Hume's constructive account, according to which moral motives and moral judgments are produced not by reason, but by the passions.

Against Self-Interest Theories

In the second *Enquiry*, Hume's "recasting" of book 3 of the *Treatise*, the critique of moral rationalism is compressed and relegated to an appendix, while Hume works harder to distinguish his own account of the foundations of morals from the self-interest theories of Hobbes and Mandeville. Hume's main objection to "the selfish hypothesis" (beside the fact that it is "contrary to common feeling") can be concisely stated: it is a trivial task to identify thousands of actions that we regard as virtuous even though we ourselves have "no real interest" in the outcome of those actions. Self-interest theorists offer explanations for our moral approval of apparently altruistic acts that are practically conspiratorial in their attempts to identify self-serving motives hidden even to those performing the acts. Hume thus considers the hypothesis that we "pursue only our private interest" to be needlessly complex when compared to his own hypothesis: we possess a "general benevolence" toward mankind such that we naturally approve of actions that benefit society in general, irrespective of whether they happen to benefit us individually.

Hume's Moral Theory

Hume's constructive account of morality is developed, as one would expect, along the lines of his "science" of human nature, and thus on a thoroughly empiricist and naturalistic foundation. Hume has no place for a morality based on divinely revealed commandments or divinely instituted natural laws and rights. What he offers instead is an innovative synthesis of *moral sentimentalism* and *virtue ethics*. Although he insists upon a modern, scientific theory of morality that moves beyond religious superstitions, Hume retains an affinity for the ancient Greco-Roman emphasis on virtues and vices as the central moral concepts (as opposed to the Judeo-Christian emphasis on divine laws). Once again, this preference reflects his commitment to naturalism over supernaturalism. Put simply, Hume argues that our moral judgments are grounded in feelings ("sentiments") of approval and disapproval about character traits that issue in particular actions. The traits we approve, we call virtues; those we disapprove, vices.

Hume's entire moral theory is founded upon the theory

of the passions set forth in book 2 of the *Treatise* ("Of the Passions"). By "passions," Hume means not merely what we normally call emotions, but also other motivating mental states, such as affections, desires, and aversions. (Recall that Hume believes the intellect has no power to move the will toward action; that power lies solely with the passions.) The passions are impressions rather than ideas (i.e., felt rather than thought), but they are "secondary" or "reflective" in nature, which is to say that they arise spontaneously in response to other impressions or ideas (*THN* 2.1.1.1–2).

As with his theory of the mind, Hume draws various distinctions between the passions. The first division is between *calm* and *violent* passions (which, like the basic distinction between ideas and impressions, is more a matter of degree than kind). The violent passions are the more forceful and frequent ones in our experience. These may be subdivided into *direct* and *indirect* passions. The six *direct* passions—desire and aversion, joy and grief, hope and fear—arise immediately from our observation or contemplation of things we regard as good or bad. When I witness the birth of my first child, for example, I experience joy; when I consider the possibility that I might be included in the next round of layoffs, I experience fear.

In contrast, the *indirect* passions—among which love, hatred, pride, and humility take center stage for Hume—arise as the consequence of more basic passions by way of a complex process involving principles of association. As I experience joy while listening to a performance of a Beethoven symphony, by a kind of causal association I will also feel love for its composer.[1]

The calm passions, on the other hand, Hume characterizes as weaker, more reflective feelings of pleasure and displeasure that

---

1. Note that for Hume love does not carry amorous connotations. He has in mind what we would now call esteem or admiration.

are triggered by our original impressions and derivative ideas. It is these nonviolent passions that Hume connects with moral and aesthetic judgments. When reflecting on the idea of giving a financial gift to an impoverished relative, I experience a sense of approval, which I associate with moral goodness or virtue. On hearing a tuneless version of "My Way" sung by a drunken businessman in a karaoke bar, I have a feeling of disapproval, which I associate with aesthetic ugliness (and perhaps also moral vice).

Book 3 of the *Treatise* ("Of Morals") extends Hume's theory of the passions into a full-blown account of moral foundations. As Hume sees matters, moral judgments are essentially judgments about virtues and vices (thus his account is a form of virtue ethics). Human actions arise from character traits or habits, which are regarded by observers with either approval (virtues) or disapproval (vices). Character traits are the primary objects of our approval and disapproval, even though we don't directly observe those traits, but instead observe people's actions and make causal inferences about their characters. When we make moral judgments about a person's actions, we are really making judgments about their character, insofar as it generated those actions.

An important component of Hume's theory is his notion of *sympathy*. As Hume defines it, sympathy isn't a feeling, but rather is a faculty or process by which we replicate in our own minds the feelings of others. Suppose I observe a young man helping an elderly lady with her groceries. I cannot directly experience her feelings of happiness. Even so, I can perceive the outward expression of her happiness and form an idea of her feelings, which in turn generates a similar feeling in my own mind, one of approval, which serves as the ground for a positive moral judgment about the young man's character. The strength of this sympathetic passion, Hume argues, will depend on the degree to which one has associative relations with the other person. Thus, if I were myself an elderly lady, or if the lady were my own mother, I would experience more pronounced feelings of approval.

Were sympathy to operate unregulated, it would lead to all manner of partisanship and prejudice because we tend to favor those with whom we closely associate. Hume wants to show that if there really are virtues and vices, they must be universally recognized. He therefore argues that general moral judgments about what constitute virtues and vices must be made from a "common point of view" (*THN* 3.3.1.30; *EPM* 9.6). This requires us not only to put ourselves "in the other person's shoes," as we say, when judging their character and actions in light of their own associative relations with others, but also to form generalized conclusions about which traits lead to actions that please (or displease) ourselves and others. Moral virtues are therefore those character traits that are *generally agreeable or useful* to ourselves and others, and conversely for moral vices.

With this analysis in place, Hume proceeds to identify various virtues (along with their opposing vices) and to explain why we consider them virtues—or at least why we *should* do so. One notable feature of his treatment is the extent to which he opposes the traditional Christian understanding of moral virtues. For example, Hume maintains that moderate pride is virtuous since it is nothing more than the proper recognition of something commendable in ourselves. The "monkish" practices of self-denial and self-flagellation, on the other hand, are not virtuous at all, since they bring no one pleasure and serve no public good.

In the concluding chapter of his second *Enquiry*, Hume summarizes the core of his theory of morals:

> Every quality of the mind, which is *useful* or *agreeable* to the *person himself* or to *others*, communicates a pleasure to the spectator, engages his esteem, and is admitted under the honorable denomination of virtue or merit. (*EPM* 9.12)

Although he eschews dogmatism in matters philosophical, Hume expresses considerable confidence in his account:

> I cannot, *at present*, be more assured of any truth, which I learn from reasoning and argument, than that personal merit consists entirely in the usefulness or agreeableness of qualities to the person himself possessed of them, or to others, who have any intercourse with him. (*EPM* 9.13)

Yet, true to form, he immediately confesses that when he reflects on the perennial debate among philosophers about the foundations of morality, he falls back on "diffidence and skepticism" and suspects that matters cannot be as obvious as they now seem to him.

In sum, what Hume offers is a naturalized theory of moral sentimentalism. The thinkers who laid the groundwork for Hume, such as Hutcheson, posited that our recognition of moral qualities arises from a divinely bestowed moral sense. Hume has no need for that hypothesis. In his view, the mere experience of moral approbation and disapprobation is sufficient grounds for morals. No further explanation is needed. Perceiving a man's virtues is as natural as perceiving the coloring of his clothes. Indeed, Hume himself makes the comparison explicit:

> Vice and virtue, therefore, may be compar'd to sounds, colours, heat and cold, which, according to modern philosophy, *are not qualities in objects, but perceptions in the mind.* (*THN* 3.1.1.26, emphasis added)

Moral attributes are thus secondary qualities, like sounds and colors. Honesty is no more an objective, mind-independent property of Abraham Lincoln than the whiteness of his shirt; strictly speaking, they are both qualities that pertain subjectively to our minds. And yet, Hume would insist, no one would deny that Lincoln's shirt really is white. Morals are as real as colors.

Thus, for Hume, the normativity of morality is grounded in nothing more than a special class of psychological qualities. To be morally good is to be generally experienced as agreeable and useful. Hume's sentimentalism is commonly characterized as a noncognitivist theory of morality because sentiments aren't propositional; a feeling as such can be neither true nor false. Thus, it is argued, there can be no moral truths, on Hume's view. It is doubtful that Hume would have accepted such a characterization, for he clearly thinks that we do make moral judgments (e.g., "The queen is kind") that can be true or false. That said, Humean moral judgments still need to be understood in terms of secondary qualities, akin to such statements as "The sky is blue" and "The water is warm" (i.e., the sky *looks* blue and the water *feels* warm).

A New Account of Justice

Any moral theory worth its salt needs to provide an account of justice. What is justice? On what basis do we make judgments about whether actions are just or unjust? Do principles of justice transcend human societies (perhaps being established by God) or are they created by those societies?

Representing the medieval scholastic view, Thomas Aquinas (1225–74) held that justice is grounded in divine law, which can be known by natural reason. Thomas Hobbes took a very different view: there is no such thing as natural justice; in reality, what we call justice is grounded in a social contract whereby a sovereign government is established to maintain law and order. In opposition to Hobbes, John Locke (1632–1704) argued that justice is a matter of natural law and natural rights, especially the right to private property. Hume takes issue with all of these approaches, offering instead an account of justice consistent with his naturalistic methodology, his empiricist epistemology, and his sentimentalist moral theory.

Central to Hume's understanding of justice is his distinction between *natural* and *artificial* virtues. Natural virtues are those that pertain to humans in a "state of nature," that is, prior to forming social institutions and governments. Such virtues include generosity, kindness, and friendliness, which are recognized in all human societies and cultures. Artificial virtues, in contrast, exist only where certain rules and institutions have been established for the sake of the public good. Understood as a virtue, justice is artificial rather than natural, according to Hume.

How then does this artificial virtue arise? In essence, it is grounded in practical rules for managing property and contracts, established solely on the basis of their public utility. Hume argues that in a state of overabundant resources, there would be no need for property laws or contractual obligations. We would simply take whatever we needed, with no harm or cost to anyone else. When resources are scarce, however, we are forced to cooperate with other people to meet our needs. Hume thinks that humans are naturally cooperative, although that tendency is restricted to our close associates (primarily family and friends). Over time, we recognize that broader cooperation with people outside our circle will be beneficial for everyone, and thus we settle upon conventions that establish property rights. Once such rights are in place, it is a natural next step for societies to establish rules governing the transfer or exchange of property, as well as laws of contract. The final step involves the establishment of governments to facilitate and enforce property rights and contractual obligations. Governments do not create property laws; rather, property laws beget governments.

Hume doesn't suggest that any of this takes place in a formal manner or by a deliberate plan. There are no councils or decrees that establish the principles of justice, nor can they be traced back to any promises or agreements. (Hume argues that promise-keeping presupposes such principles and therefore cannot ground them.) Rather, the rules of justice arise organically as the fruit of human societies seeking to cooperate for the utility of all, underwritten by a natural human benevolence. Hume's account of justice is thus, like that of Hobbes, conventionalist in nature; contra Hobbes, however, it involves no social contracts or appeals to self-interest.

In what sense then is justice a virtue? In this sense: justice, as an artificial virtue, is nothing more than that character trait (or set of traits) which leads people to observe the practical rules of justice—to honor property rights, to deal honestly and fairly with others, to maintain contracts, and to submit to the rule of law. When we observe someone acting in accordance with these rules, we approve of their character, which is just to say that we deem them morally virtuous.

Hume's theory of justice is thus both evolutionary, in the sense that justice naturally evolves out of social relations and needs, and utilitarian, in the sense that rules of justice are a function of general social usefulness. On the latter point, Hume is explicit:

> That Justice is useful to society, and consequently that *part* of its merit, at least, must arise from that consideration, it would be a superfluous undertaking to prove. That public utility is the *sole* origin of justice, and that reflections on the beneficial consequences of this virtue are the *sole* foundation of its merit; this proposition, being more curious and important, will better deserve our examination and enquiry. (*EPM* 3.1)

> Thus, the rules of equity or justice depend entirely on the particular state and condition, in which men are placed, and owe

their origin and existence to that *utility*, which results to the public from their strict and regular observance. (*EPM* 3.12)

Hence the ideas of property become necessary in all civil society: Hence justice derives its usefulness to the public: And hence alone arises its merit and moral obligation. (*EPM* 3.13)

Hume believes that his theory of justice, like his theory of morals, can be established solely "by following the experimental method" (*EPM* 1.10)—that is, by reflection on our own ideas and motives, combined with general observations about human behavior—all without any reference to questionable metaphysical or theological theses.

4

HUME'S RELIGIOUS SKEPTICISM

It appears that Hume abandoned any serious commitment to religion as a young man, if ever there was such a commitment. His mother was a devoted Scots Presbyterian, his uncle pastored the local church he attended as a child, and he would almost certainly have been familiar with the Westminster Catechisms. But for whatever reason, David neither inherited nor embraced the family faith.

To the extent that Hume had any religious inclinations, they amounted to little more than a preoccupation with moral piety. James Boswell reports that the young Hume studied *The Whole Duty of Man*, a popular Protestant devotional work, drew from it a long list of vices, and, after examining himself, decided that he had "no inclination to commit them."[1] By his own confession, Hume found it odd to be enjoined to suppress the supposed vice

---

1. Quoted in James A. Harris, *Hume: An Intellectual Biography* (Cambridge: Cambridge University Press, 2015), 49.

of pride, given that his academic abilities clearly exceeded those of his fellow students.

Hume's interest in Christianity was thus limited to its recommendation of a virtuous life; even at this early stage, his approach to religion was naturalistic. During his university years, he was drawn to the ancient Greco-Roman account of the virtues, rather than that of Christianity. During this period, he also embarked on a close examination of natural theology to determine whether the doctrines of Christianity could be established on rational grounds. This only led him further away from religious faith. According to Boswell, Hume "never had entertained any belief in religion since he began to read [John] Locke and [Samuel] Clarke." Since both men were renowned for their defenses of natural theology, the clear implication is that Hume was unimpressed by their arguments.[2]

It would only be a slight exaggeration to say that Hume's entire career was spent, in one way or another, in defense of his religious skepticism. On every subject he addresses—history, politics, economics, ethics, psychology, and even religion—Hume's working assumption is that it can be adequately explained without reference to any supernatural sources or causes. Furthermore, Hume offers four general lines of argument aimed at destabilizing and discrediting traditional religious claims: (1) his general skeptical stance toward "divinity or school metaphysics," as expressed in the famous conclusion of the first book of the *Treatise*; (2) his naturalistic account of the history of religion; (3) his critique of natural theology, forcefully expressed in his *Dialogues concerning Natural Religion*; and (4) his influential argument against miracles in section 10 of the first *Enquiry*.

Concerning the first of these lines of argument, little more needs to be said, except perhaps to make one observation:

2. Ibid., 50–51.

Hume could have stated more explicitly that, according to his theory of ideas, it would be impossible in principle to form an intelligible idea of the God of the Bible, since we never enjoy original impressions of such a being. (If the idea of an external world of material objects is of dubious intelligibility, as Hume believed, there is no question that a transcendent, immaterial reality would be equally problematic.) In this chapter, we will therefore focus on the other three pillars of his case against the Christian religion.

Religion Naturalized

Even the irreligious need to give an account of religion. Why do so many people hold religious beliefs, and why those religious beliefs? How did religion arise in the first place?

Hume is committed by his overall project to offering a naturalistic account of religious beliefs and practices. This he attempts in his essay "The Natural History of Religion," which appeared in his *Four Dissertations* (1757). Three theses stand out: (1) The origin and diversity of religion can be explained on a naturalistic basis. (2) Religious beliefs typically arise, not from rational or empirical considerations, but from cruder human instincts. (3) Religion was originally polytheistic rather than monotheistic. Only the last of these could be fairly regarded as a novel contribution by Hume to the debates of his day.

Hume takes the heart of religion to be "a universal propensity to believe in an invisible, intelligent power" that acts within our world (*NHR* 15.5). Religious beliefs are fueled by a crude inference of design, drawn from the order and beauty we observe in the world. However, this inference is not nearly adequate to support anything like "genuine theism," that is, belief in a single, supreme deity who possesses all perfections. For Hume, such a refined religious view came late in history. On the contrary, "polytheism or idolatry was, and must have been, the first and most ancient religion of mankind" (*NHR* 1.1). This is clearly opposed to the biblical narrative, according to which the first humans were monotheists and descended into idolatrous, polytheistic practices only after the fall of Adam. Hume's simple argument for his thesis is that if monotheism could be effortlessly deduced by reason from the natural order, it would have held such a grip on men's minds as to preclude the development of polytheism.[3]

According to Hume's account, polytheism arose out of the fear and ignorance of primitive people. Afraid of the various threats to their well-being and unable to discern the true (natural) causes of the calamities that befell them, they transformed the "invisible, intelligent power" into a pantheon of anthropomorphic deities who could be swayed by acts of devotion and sacrifice—or so they hoped. As gods were invented to explain and "solve" the natural trials of life—drought, warfare, infertility, and so on—so the pantheon proliferated.

How then did monotheism arise? Hume's core argument is that the psychological forces that gave rise to polytheistic religion were sooner or later countered by other human tendencies, specifically a "propensity for adulation." Even idolaters tend to concentrate their worship and adoration on one particular deity that they take to be their god, over against the gods of their rivals and enemies. Over time, these henotheists increasingly exalt the attributes of that deity until it eventually eclipses all others: the parochial god becomes the "one true God" who alone possesses all powers and perfections.

Yet this evolution of religion isn't an advancement, in Hume's view. He is insistent that monotheism isn't built upon

---

3. Note that Hume's conclusion would follow only if reason governed the passions—something he famously denies in his other works.

philosophical arguments, but rather the same kind of "irrational and superstitious opinions" as gave rise to polytheism. Insofar as religious monotheism coincides with philosophical theism, it is "by chance . . . not by reason" (*NHR* 6.5). Nor is this monotheism a stable conviction. Rather, the human passions that gave rise to polytheism continue to push back in that direction, resulting in continual fluctuations over the course of human history. Our experience of suffering and chaos in the world drives the polytheistic impulse, while our propensity to simplify causes and to fix our adoration on a perfect and singular deity pushes us toward monotheism. In Hume's view, there is no rational way to adjudicate between these two poles, because each is driven by passions, rather than reason. Indeed, in the latter sections of the "Natural History," both polytheistic and monotheistic superstitions (such as the Catholic doctrine of the real presence) are subjected to ridicule. Precisely because monotheism enjoys a modicum of philosophical respectability, its corruption by the religious is all the more tragic. In the end, neither religious scheme can be considered superior. Hume's conclusion, predictably enough, is that we ought to suspend judgment altogether about the particulars of religion.

In all of this, Hume is careful never to deny the existence of God or to imply directly that any of the articles of the Christian faith are false. He presents his case as a disinterested observer offering an explanatory hypothesis, even though there can be no doubt that the argument is calculated to erode confidence in the biblical account of religion. Nevertheless, Hume's argument shouldn't trouble Christian believers for the simple reason that it begs the question entirely. Hume simply takes for granted that the Old Testament narratives cannot be treated as historically reliable (never mind divinely inspired), and his entire methodology is driven by his naturalistic presuppositions. Far from taking a neutral, scientific approach (unless "scientific" is defined in his own prejudicial terms), Hume is engaged in the project of explaining the phenomenon of religion in terms of a world-view to which he is already committed. He is free to do so, of course, but the same freedom should be extended to orthodox Christians who have their own (very different) presuppositions.

Hume's Critique of Natural Theology

In the eighteenth century, *natural religion* was commonly distinguished from *revealed religion*. Natural religion concerns what may be known about God and his purposes from nature alone, that is, through unaided natural reason and empirical observations of the natural world. Revealed religion, on the other hand, considers putative sources of special revelation, such as divinely inspired prophets and miraculous signs. Hume pioneered what are now considered to be among the most influential critiques of both forms of religion. His critique of revealed religion centers on his arguments against miracles, which we will consider in the next section. Hume's objections to natural theology appear in various places, but the most systematic critique comes in his famous *Dialogues concerning Natural Religion*. It seems that Hume began working on the *Dialogues* around the same time as "The Natural History of Religion," but was counseled by his friends not to publish it during his lifetime, due to its controversial content. Hume made several revisions of the work before his death, leaving it to his nephew to arrange for its publication in 1779.

The *Dialogues* features three main characters: Demea, the religious rationalist; Cleanthes, the religious empiricist; and Philo, the philosophical skeptic. In keeping with his rationalism, Demea favors an *a priori* cosmological proof of God's existence, according to which a necessary first cause can be deduced with logical certainty from the contingent existence of

the universe. While Demea holds that God's existence is rationally indisputable, he tends toward mysticism regarding God's
attributes, including his moral attributes. He is highly critical of
what he takes to be Cleanthes' anthropomorphic view of God,
which seemingly denies God's perfection and infinitude. Many
commentators hold that Demea is modeled on the influential
philosopher-theologian Samuel Clarke (1675–1729), whose
version of the cosmological argument was widely regarded as
the gold standard in Hume's day, although Clarke was much
more confident in his knowledge of the divine attributes than
Demea.[4] In any event, Demea is meant to represent the theologically orthodox philosopher.

Cleanthes is critical of Demea's rationalistic approach and
prefers a version of the design argument, reasoning on analogy
with human artifacts that the order and function observed in
nature points us to some divine intelligence or architect behind
the universe itself. Cleanthes leans heavily on the principle that
there must be a degree of similarity between an effect and its
cause, a principle that Hume disputes elsewhere (in his general
analysis of causation) and attacks in the *Dialogues* (at least in the
way it is applied to natural religion).

It is generally agreed that Philo serves as Hume's primary
mouthpiece in this work, although Philo keeps his cards close to
his chest. His strategy is to raise critical questions about the arguments that Demea and Cleanthes use to justify their religious
convictions, but he also effectively plays the two theists against
one another, allowing their deep disagreements to vindicate his
own skeptical position indirectly.

Notably, at no point in the *Dialogues* is the existence of God
considered to be in doubt. The introduction concedes that there

---

4. In *DNR* 9, where the *a priori* argument is discussed, Demea quotes directly
from Clarke.

is no truth "so obvious, so certain, as the being of a God," and the three participants agree that the being of God is "unquestionable and self-evident" (*DNR* 2.3). The debate concerns the *nature* of God, that is, what can be known by reason and observation about the attributes of God. That God's existence is conceded turns out to be small consolation, however, since the answer to the latter question turns out to be: virtually nothing. "God" is thus a lightweight term for Hume, denoting no more than the cause (or causes) of the order in the universe.

The *Dialogues* is a complex and subtle work, and space forbids a detailed exposition. We will therefore focus on those elements that are generally regarded as having had the greatest impact: (1) Hume's objections to the *a priori* cosmological argument, (2) his dismantling of the analogical design argument, and (3) his discussion of the problem of evil and its implications for our knowledge of God's moral attributes.[5]

Speaking through Demea, Hume summarizes the cosmological argument as follows:

> Whatever exists must have a cause or reason of its existence; it being absolutely impossible for any thing to produce itself, or be the cause of its own existence. In mounting up, therefore, from effects to causes, we must either go on in tracing an infinite succession, without any ultimate cause at all, or must at last have recourse to some ultimate cause, that is *necessarily* existent. (*DNR* 9.3)

The argument is attacked from several angles. One indirect criticism is found in the *Treatise*, where Hume challenges the principle that whatever comes into existence must have a cause of

---

5. Hume conflates the ontological and cosmological arguments, treating them in effect as one *a priori* argument for a necessarily existent (or self-existent) being.

its existence (*THN* 1.3.3). From a strictly empiricist standpoint, it is impossible to establish *a priori* any necessary truths about causation. For all we know, some things can come into existence without any cause; there is no contradiction in the idea itself, and therefore it must be possible.[6] Hence, the cosmological argument is based upon a highly questionable principle of causation.

In the *Dialogues*, further objections are raised. First, the very idea of "necessary existence" is problematic. Any claimed existence is a matter of fact—recall Hume's Fork—and thus cannot be proven by any *a priori* deduction. Moreover, any purported matter of fact can be denied without self-contradiction, and thus the notion of a necessary existence is incoherent: "Whatever we conceive as existent, we can also conceive as non-existent. There is no being, therefore, whose non-existence implies a contradiction." (This also serves, incidentally, as Hume's refutation of Anselm's ontological argument.)

In any event, even if one accepts that something could enjoy necessary existence, why not simply ascribe that property to the material universe and leave it at that? If something has to exist necessarily, would it not be simpler to posit that the universe exists necessarily? What need then for the Deity?

One common objection to the cosmological argument is that there is nothing inherently contradictory about an infinite chain of contingent causes stretching back into eternity past, with no initial, uncaused cause. Clarke offered the following response to the objection: even if every member of the series could be explained in terms of some preceding member as its cause, that would still leave unexplained the cause of the whole chain. Hume dismisses this response in one brief paragraph by suggesting that once we have explained what causes all the parts of a whole, we

---

6. Recall that for Hume, conceivability without logical contradiction entails possibility.

have thereby explained the cause of the whole. Nothing remains to be explained.

Hume's core objection to the cosmological argument is its *a priori* nature. The design argument is a different beast, however, since it relies on reasoning from observable features of the universe to some intelligent agency. It is an empirical effect-to-cause argument. Hume's strategy is to show that the analogical reasoning employed by Cleanthes is simply too weak to establish the kind of robust monotheism that Christianity represents. As we noted earlier, Hume concedes that the universe bears the marks of design and purpose, and that it is natural to believe it has an intelligent cause. The problem is that specific hypotheses about this cause cannot be determined by our observational data.

In the first place, while we have considerable experience of human agents producing different artifacts, we have observed only one universe and we have never observed the cause of a universe. Inferences about the cause of the universe based on an entirely different class of causes and effects (i.e., human artifacts) are highly unreliable, suggests Hume. Moreover, even if we grant that such an inference is possible, we are in no position to infer a single, infinite creator; if we want to infer similarities between the causes of artifacts (e.g., buildings) and the cause of the universe, we ought to conclude that the latter is also the product of multiple agents who are finite, temporal, and corporeal. But that would be theologically unorthodox.

The matter is further complicated by the fact that the universe is far from perfect. There is considerable suffering, as well as happiness, and many things in the world appear to be dysfunctional or broken. Imperfections in the effect surely imply imperfections in the cause. At one point, Hume playfully suggests that, for all we know, our universe is the product of "some infant deity, who afterwards abandoned it, ashamed of his lame performance" (*DNR* 5.12).

Hume's general point is this: he who lives by the analogical sword will also die by it. If we are invited to reason from effect to cause in proportion to the available evidence, there is no hope of showing that the cause must be a single, perfect, infinite, spiritual being. The empirical evidence is consistent with a limitless number of competing hypotheses. In any case, the entire enterprise of teleological argumentation can only lead to an objectionably anthropomorphic God—a deity who is merely a smarter, stronger version of a human agent.

Even if we grant the existence of an intelligent cause behind the universe, the question remains whether we can infer that this cause is morally good. Hume not only challenges the inference, but also offers a positive argument against the idea of a morally perfect God. In part 10 of the *Dialogues*, Demea suggests that people are more commonly driven to religion by the abundant miseries of this world than by philosophical reasoning. After a discussion of the multifarious ills to which mankind is subject, Philo crystalizes the dilemma for the theist with a classic statement of the philosophical problem posed by the existence of evil in the world:

> Is [the Deity] willing to prevent evil, but not able? Then he is impotent. Is he able, but not willing? Then he is malevolent. Is he both able and willing? Whence then is evil? (*DNR* 10.15)

The conundrum is clear. If God were both all-powerful and all-good, he would be willing and able to prevent evil. Since evil exists, it seems we must deny either his power or his goodness.

Demea's response to the problem is essentially to retreat into theological mysticism: he rejects Cleanthes' anthropomorphic view of God (and thus his empirical approach to natural theology) and suggests that our knowledge of the world is simply too limited to make any inferences about God's goodness. For all we know, the "present evil phenomena . . . are rectified in other regions, and in some future period of existence." Cleanthes sticks to his guns and insists that we must deny that, as a matter of observed fact, the miseries of this world outweigh its joys. Philo simply observes that Cleanthes has no hope of defending this claim, and thus he too must admit skepticism regarding the creator's moral attributes. Yet such skepticism would leave us without any "just foundation for religion" (*DNR* 10.33).

The debate continues in part 11, where Philo raises further objections to Cleanthes' position. Cleanthes suggests that the problem of evil may be alleviated if we suppose "the Author of Nature to be finitely perfect" and engaged in a forced trade-off between goods and evils. Philo responds by identifying four kinds of natural evil, each of which even a finite deity would be able to prevent or significantly alleviate. Pushing Cleanthes to be consistent with his own empirical method, Philo argues that of four possible hypotheses regarding the causes of the universe— (1) they're perfectly good; (2) they're perfectly evil; (3) they're both good and evil; (4) they're indifferent to good and evil—the fourth "seems by far the most probable" with respect to all of our evidence.

Hume's overall strategy, in his discussion of the problem of evil, is to use Demea and Cleanthes (with Philo serving as middleman) to pose an intolerable dilemma for the theist: either (1) follow the *a priori* approach of Demea, positing an infinite God whose moral relationship with the world is utterly mysterious and inscrutable, and thus removing any basis for revealed religion, or (2) follow the empiricism of Cleanthes and settle for an anthropomorphic deity (or pantheon of deities) indifferent to the miseries we endure. Neither of these, as Hume well knows, will be appealing to an orthodox Christian.

In the end, Hume's critique of natural theology boils down to this. The *rationalist* approach is a dead end: God's existence cannot be established *a priori*, and even if it could, such a God would be too distant and unlike us to serve as the proper object of religious devotion. The only alternative is an *empiricist* approach, but our actual observations of the world cannot support an inference of a single, perfect Deity. The most we can justifiably conclude is that there is some intelligent cause of the universe. Beyond that, nothing more can be reliably established.

Hume's Argument against Miracles

Hume objected to revealed religion on multiple grounds, but the centerpiece of his critique is his celebrated argument against miracles in section 10 of *An Enquiry concerning Human Understanding*. His working assumption, shared by his contemporaries, is that any revealed religion—and certainly Christianity— would have to be founded on credible evidence of miraculous events that somehow confirmed its central doctrines. Hume was transparently pleased with his argument, which he touted as a kind of all-purpose, knock-down refutation of the miraculous: "an everlasting check to all kinds of superstitious delusion and . . . useful as long as the world endures." Hume had conceived of the argument much earlier in his career and originally planned to include it in the *Treatise*, but apparently decided it would be too controversial to publish at that time. By 1748, Hume's reputation as an infidel was sufficiently established to make its inclusion less hazardous.

"Of Miracles" consists of two parts. In the first, Hume presents his central argument against miracles—more specifically, against believing any testimony that a miraculous event occurred. Although never explicitly stated, it is clear that the primary target of Hume's argument is the apostolic testimony about the resurrection of Jesus. The second part of the essay presents four further reasons for skepticism about reported miracles.

There has been considerable debate among commentators on two points: (1) how Hume's primary argument should be interpreted, and what he thinks it establishes, and (2) how the subsidiary arguments of part 2 relate to the primary argument of part 1. One reason for the debate is that, on the most straightforward reading, if Hume's opening argument were sound, it would render his subsequent arguments entirely superfluous. To simplify matters, I will adopt what I regard as the most plausible interpretation of Hume's arguments. By this I mean not the most defensible formulations of the arguments themselves, but rather how Hume himself most likely understood the arguments, given what he actually wrote and how he subsequently responded to his critics.

The lynchpin of Hume's argument is the following maxim: "A wise man . . . proportions his belief to the evidence" (*EHU* 10.4). The basic idea is plausible enough: whenever we consider any claim, we must weigh the supporting evidence against the opposing evidence and proportion our credence accordingly. If the evidence for the claim strongly outweighs the evidence against it, we may confidently believe that the claim is true; if the reverse is the case, we may confidently disbelieve the claim. If the evidence for and against cancel each other out, however, we should simply suspend judgment.

Also crucial to Hume's argument is a distinction between two types of evidence: *proof* and *probability*. If I have consistently observed one event following another event (e.g., water freezing when the temperature drops below 0°C) without a single exception, then I have proof that I will observe the same conjunction of events in the future. If, on the other hand, I have encountered some contrary observations, then I possess only probability with respect to future observations.

With these building blocks in place, Hume develops the following principled objection to reported miracles: in such cases, the evidence against the actual occurrence of the miracle will inevitably swamp the evidence for it, no matter how respectable the testimony to the miracle may be. This is so because Hume defines a miracle as "a violation of the laws of nature."[7] What distinguishes a miraculous event (such as a resurrection from the dead) from a merely marvelous event (such as a surprising recovery from a serious illness) is that the former is deemed to be contrary to the laws of nature. Now our observational evidence is that there are no exceptions to the laws of nature, so this amounts to proof, not merely probability, that a miracle did not occur. Consequently, no countervailing evidence of any kind could be strong enough to overturn it. As Hume triumphantly declares:

> As a firm and unalterable experience has established these laws [of nature], the proof against a miracle, from the very nature of the fact, is as entire as any argument from experience can possibly be imagined. . . . There must, therefore, be a uniform experience against every miraculous event, otherwise the event would not merit that appellation. And as an [*sic*] uniform experience amounts to a proof, there is here a direct and full *proof*, from the nature of the fact, against the existence of any miracle; nor can such a proof be destroyed, or the miracle rendered credible, but by an opposite proof, which is superior. (*EHU* 10.12, emphasis original)

In other words, since our uniform experience of the world furnishes us with proof against any claim that the laws of nature have been violated, only a "superior" and "opposite" proof could give us rational grounds to believe any claim that a miracle has

---

7. In a note, Hume adds, "A miracle may be accurately defined, *a transgression of a law of nature by a particular volition of the Deity, or by the interposition of some invisible agent.*" For the purposes of his argument, the additional qualification of divine agency is irrelevant.

occurred. But proof is by Hume's definition the strongest type of evidence, and thus a superior opposing proof is impossible. In short, no evidence in principle could justify believing any claim that a miracle has occurred.

In part 1, Hume allows, as a bare theoretical possibility, that testimonial evidence for a miracle could amount to "an entire proof." But in part 2 he bolsters his case by giving four reasons why this concession is "too liberal":

1. "There is not to be found, in all history, any miracle attested by a sufficient number of men, of such unquestioned good-sense, education, and learning" that we could safely rule out delusion or deliberate deception.
2. Humans have a natural tendency to find pleasure in surprise and wonder, and thus to be more credulous when it comes to reported miracles.
3. Claims that miracles have occurred typically abound "among ignorant and barbarous nations" where people lack scientific knowledge.
4. The miracles alleged by the adherents of different religions and sects serve to cancel each other out. People readily believe the miracles associated with their own religious tradition, while expressing incredulity toward those of other traditions. This suggests a lack of intellectual integrity across all traditions.

The upshot of Hume's observations is that our actual testimonial evidence for miracles comes nowhere near the level required to overcome our proofs of complete regularity of the laws of nature:

> Upon the whole, then, it appears, that no testimony for any kind of miracle has ever amounted to a probability, much less to a proof. (*EHU* 10.35)

True to form, Hume concludes his critique with a rhetorical flourish wrapped in a mantle of feigned piety:

> We may conclude, that the *Christian Religion* not only was at first attended with miracles, but even at this day cannot be believed by any reasonable person without one. Mere reason is insufficient to convince us of its veracity: And whoever is moved by *Faith* to assent to it, is conscious of a continued miracle in his own person, which subverts all the principles of his understanding, and gives him a determination to believe what is most contrary to custom and experience. (*EHU* 10.41)

Put less delicately: if a miracle is a violation of the laws of nature, then any religious faith based on a miracle is a violation of the laws of reason.

Was Hume an Atheist?

It is evident from his attacks on religion that Hume was not a Christian believer or indeed a theist of any kind. Should we consider him a full-blown atheist?[8] Modern atheists are understandably eager to claim him for their cause, but the question has been subject to considerable scholarly debate. There are two good reasons to refrain from designating Hume an atheist. The first is that his own expressed skepticism about metaphysical claims seems to preclude it. Hume holds that metaphysical propositions are always speculative and unsupported by the evidence;

8. I use the term *atheist* here in the traditional sense: one who believes that God does not exist, as opposed to one who merely lacks belief that God exists. For useful discussions of the distinction between atheism and agnosticism, see Paul Draper, "Atheism and Agnosticism," in *The Stanford Encyclopedia of Philosophy*, ed. Edward N. Zalta, Fall 2017, https://plato.stanford.edu/archives/fall2017/entries/atheism -agnosticism/; Graham Oppy, *Atheism and Agnosticism*, Elements in the Philosophy of Religion (Cambridge: Cambridge University Press, 2018).

based on experience alone, we cannot reasonably affirm either theism or atheism (where the latter is understood as the denial of God's existence).

The second complication comes from the fact that in several works Hume expresses the opinion that the natural universe bears the marks of some kind of intelligent cause. For example:

> The whole frame of nature bespeaks an intelligent author; and no rational enquirer can, after serious reflection, suspend his belief a moment with regard to the primary principles of genuine Theism and Religion. (*NHR* Intro.1)

Similarly, at the end of the *Dialogues*, he backs away from an unqualified religious skepticism. Some commentators argue that this was a deliberate and somewhat disingenuous strategy on Hume's part, concealing the true extent of his skepticism, due to the opprobrium directed at atheists in eighteenth-century Britain. However, Hume's criticisms of religion during his lifetime were bold enough, and there was no need to pull his punches in the *Dialogues*, since he had arranged for them to be published posthumously.

All things considered, it is probably best to view Hume as a skeptical deist who held loosely to the idea of an intelligent cause behind the universe, yet recoiled from making any specific claims about the nature of that cause. Any belief in a cosmic architect Hume would most likely have credited to his natural instinct, rather than to reason. At the same time, it would be fair to describe him as a practical atheist, given that his approach to life was conducted on an entirely naturalistic basis, with no regard for any deity or deities.

5

HUME'S CONTINUING
RELEVANCE

The significance of Hume's thought, like that of many influential philosophers, was not widely recognized in his day. Only generations later did the impact of his arguments become evident. With the benefit of hindsight, we can now see the full range of Hume's influence on subsequent philosophical thought and contemporary secular culture. In this chapter, we will note five areas where the impact of Hume's philosophical project can be clearly seen today.

The Kantian Turn

The importance of the German philosopher Immanuel Kant (1724–1804) in the history of Western thought can hardly be disputed. Yet without Hume, there would have been no Kant. Early in his career, Kant took a rationalist stance in the line of G. W. Leibniz (1646–1716) and Christian Wolff (1679–1754), attempting to build an entire metaphysical system by deduction from a relatively small number of *a priori* truths of reason. But an earthquake shook Kant's world when he encountered the works of Hume. As Kant himself famously put it, Hume interrupted his "dogmatic slumber."[1]

Kant felt the force of Hume's critique of rationalist metaphysics and came to accept the empiricist axiom that factual knowledge of the world can only come through sense experience. Pure reason simply cannot deliver substantive metaphysical conclusions. At the same time, however, Kant was troubled by Hume's skeptical conclusions with respect to science (e.g., that we cannot really know objective laws of nature) and religion. According to Hume's Fork, only two kinds of beliefs can amount to knowledge: *relations of ideas* and *matters of fact*. Kant referred to these, respectively, as *analytic a priori* truths (knowable prior to sense experience merely through the analysis of ideas) and *synthetic a posteriori* truths (factual information about the world knowable only on the basis of sense experience). Kant recognized that for science to be possible, we must also have access to a *third* category: *synthetic a priori* truths. Such truths would include the laws of nature (i.e., truths about causal necessities in the natural world), arithmetical and geometrical propositions (such as the Euclidean axioms), and commonsense principles that we generally take for granted in our experience (e.g., that every event has a cause). Hume's Fork needed a third prong.

As Kant saw matters, then, the central question of metaphysics comes down to this: "How are synthetic *a priori* judgments possible?"[2] Kant's groundbreaking answer, set forth in his *Critique of Pure Reason*, is complex and decidedly obscure at points, but centers on the idea that the human mind isn't a passive blank slate

---

1. Immanuel Kant, *Prolegomena to Any Future Metaphysics* (1783), §10.
2. Immanuel Kant, *Critique of Pure Reason* (1781; rev. 1787), B19.

in receiving information through the senses, as Hume and his fellow empiricists tended to assume. Instead, the mind actively shapes and structures the raw data of sense experience so as to present us with an intelligible experience of an orderly material world. Concepts such as space, time, causality, and necessity do not refer to features "out there" in a mind-independent world to be discovered by empirical observation. If that were the case, Humean skepticism would be unavoidable. On the contrary, these concepts are intrinsic structures of the mind that are *necessarily imposed* upon experience and thus become the *preconditions* of our knowledge of a spatiotemporal world of material objects. This is Kant's "Copernican revolution": the center of the epistemological universe is not a mind-independent world, but rather a world-structuring mind. Knowledge consists not in the mind conforming to the natural world (as Hume assumed), but in the natural world conforming to the mind.

How then can synthetic *a priori* truths, such as "Every event has a cause" and "Objects exert a gravitational force proportional to their mass," be known? Simply put, by using the mind to discern the conceptual structure of the mind itself. To be more specific, Kant suggests that we can employ a powerful kind of argument known as a *transcendental argument* to identify the ideas that must be presupposed for us to have intelligible experience of an external world. While these ideas are not logical truisms, neither are they observed empirically to be true (as Hume assumed they would have to be). Instead, they are preconditions of any empirical knowledge.

Kant's response to Hume came at a price. One consequence of Kant's scheme is that human reason is strictly limited to the *phenomenal* world (that is, the world as experienced by us), and human knowledge is restricted to matters of science. The *noumenal* world—the world as it is in itself, independent of our experience—is strictly unknowable. Moreover, anything that isn't a phenomenal object, such as God or the soul, cannot be an object of knowledge.

The implications of Kant's epistemology for orthodox Christian beliefs should not be missed. On the Kantian view, traditional theological claims—whether of natural theology or revealed theology—must be either rejected or radically reconstrued. The premodern notions of divine revelation and divine action are ruled out in principle as breaches of the noumenal-phenomenal divide. Theology, unlike science, can no longer be a matter of public knowledge. It would be only a modest exaggeration to say that the modern conception of religion as a strictly private matter can be laid at the feet of Kant. Yet the feet of Kant were shod by Hume.[3]

Utilitarianism

"The greatest happiness for the greatest number is the foundation of morals and legislation," asserted Jeremy Bentham, the pioneer of modern utilitarian ethics. Bentham (1748–1832) dubbed this the "principle of utility," according to which the moral rightness or wrongness of an action is determined by whether it tends to increase or decrease overall human happiness. Bentham's theory of ethics was formulated in conscious opposition to the classical theories of natural law and natural rights, the latter of which he notoriously described as "nonsense on stilts."

While there were many precursors to Bentham's approach, from the ethical hedonism of the ancient Greeks to the "moral sense theorists" of the early eighteenth century, one of the major influences on Bentham was Hume's sentimentalist theory of

3. For further discussion of the impact of Hume and Kant on modern theology, especially Protestant liberalism, see John M. Frame, *A History of Western Philosophy and Theology* (Phillipsburg, NJ: P&R Publishing, 2015).

morals and his utilitarian account of justice. Bentham sought to develop an entirely naturalistic account of ethics, and to that end he proposed to ground moral judgments in human sensations of pleasure and pain, just as Hume had done:

> Nature has placed mankind under the governance of two sovereign masters, *pain* and *pleasure*. It is for them alone to point out what we ought to do, as well as to determine what we shall do.[4]

Following Hume, Bentham rejected the idea of God-given natural laws and rights, seeking instead to defend the justness of societal regulations on the grounds of their usefulness to mankind. Hume's assertion that "public utility is the *sole* origin of justice" could just as well have flowed from the pen of Bentham. While there are significant differences between Hume's ethics and Bentham's—for example, Bentham's theory centers on moral actions, whereas Hume's centers on moral virtues—they share the same naturalistic motivations and foundations. Bentham's approach is essentially a more consistent and streamlined version of Hume's.

Bentham's utilitarianism was further developed by his disciple John Stuart Mill (arguably in a less consistent fashion) and served as the foundation for the classical liberal approach to government. Utilitarianism, whether or not it is recognized as such, is arguably the most popular secular approach to ethics today. How can abortion be morally justified? Because the alternative would bring about greater unhappiness for all parties involved. Why should physician-assisted suicide be supported? For the same reason: if not to maximize pleasure, then at least to minimize pain. Why should we recognize and support animal

---

4. Jeremy Bentham, *An Introduction to the Principles of Morals and Legislation* (1789; rev. 1823).

rights? Because, as utilitarian ethicist Peter Singer has forcefully argued, animals experience pleasure and pain just as humans do, and thus the moral sphere encompasses us all equally. Even in this regard, Singer was anticipated by Hume (*THN* 1.3.16, 2.1.12).

Sam Harris, the influential New Atheist writer and speaker, wrote *The Moral Landscape* to counter the claim that while science can explain many things in our experience, it cannot explain morality and thus cannot provide moral direction.[5] Although Harris distances himself from Hume, specifically taking issue with the latter's dictum that one cannot derive an *ought* from an *is*, the irony is that Harris's general project (a purely scientific account of human nature) and approach to ethics (a somewhat crude version of utilitarianism) is Humean to its core. The shadow cast by Hume across the moral landscape of the twenty-first century is long and wide.

Logical Positivism and Scientism

In the 1920s, a group of philosophers and scientists known as the Vienna Circle began to develop and propound a radically empiricist approach to knowledge.[6] These logical positivists, as they later became known, essentially rehabilitated Hume's Fork: they explicitly rejected the Kantian idea of synthetic *a priori* knowledge, insisting that a rigorous scientific approach to knowledge should consist only of analytic *a priori* (i.e., purely logical) claims and synthetic *a posteriori* (i.e., observational, factual) claims. The movement was even more radically antimetaphysical than Hume had been. Whereas Hume concluded that

5. Sam Harris, *The Moral Landscape: How Science Can Determine Human Values* (New York: Free Press, 2010).

6. Led by Moritz Schlick, the group included Philipp Frank, Hans Hahn, Otto Neurath, Kurt Gödel, and Rudolf Carnap, among many others.

metaphysical theories are necessarily speculative and cannot be proven, the logical positivists argued that metaphysical claims are cognitively meaningless. For Hume, such claims might turn out be true, but no one could ever know; for the logical positivists, such claims couldn't even be false, because they have no meaningful propositional content. The basis for this dismissal was their vaunted "verificationist theory of meaning," which stipulates that statements have meaning only if they are verifiable (unless they are true by definition). Following Hume, the logical positivists held that statements of fact can only be verified empirically. Since metaphysical claims cannot be empirically verified, they must be deemed meaningless. In this way, the entire history of metaphysics from Plato to Hegel could be swept into the trash can.

Popularized by A. J. Ayer's book *Language, Truth and Logic,* logical positivism promised a thorough cleansing of both philosophy and the sciences.[7] It didn't deliver, and it didn't last. Put bluntly, it was the philosophical equivalent of decapitation as a cure for a headache. Not only were the implications of logical positivism highly counterintuitive, it rendered ethics as vacuous as metaphysics and collapsed under the weight of its self-contradictions. As many have noted (and some within the movement eventually admitted) the verificationist theory of meaning makes claims that, according to the theory itself, ought to be dismissed as meaningless.

Nevertheless, while few today would identify with logical positivism, the spirit of the movement lives on in the form of *scientism*, which in its stronger formulations reduces all knowledge to scientific knowledge and dismisses as meaningless any

7. Ayer openly declared his debt to Hume: "The views which are put forward in this treatise derive from the views of Bertrand Russell and Wittgenstein, which are themselves the logical outcome of the empiricism of Berkeley and David Hume" (Alfred Jules Ayer, *Language, Truth and Logic,* 2nd ed. [London: Victor Gollancz, 1946], 31).

questions not susceptible to scientific answers.[8] Whenever one encounters the prejudice that theological statements are nonsensical because they are unverifiable, the ghost of Hume can be found lurking in the rafters.

Naturalized Epistemology

We noted earlier that Hume is less concerned with traditional epistemological questions (such as "What is knowledge?" and "On what basis are our beliefs justified?") than with offering a naturalistic account of our ideas and beliefs: how our beliefs are formed, and why we think as we do. Most of the first book of the *Treatise* and the first *Enquiry* are taken up with issues that are more properly psychological than epistemological. This is entirely in keeping with Hume's broader project, that of developing a purely "scientific" account of human nature, with particular focus on human beliefs and actions.

Here as elsewhere, Hume was well ahead of the game. The philosopher W. V. Quine published a seminal essay in 1969 entitled "Epistemology Naturalized."[9] Exactly what Quine proposed in the essay continues to be debated, but the received view is that he was recommending (or perhaps surrendering to) a radical reorientation of the entire discipline of epistemology. The traditional position, as Quine described it, views philosophy as logically prior to science. Science has to proceed on an empirical *a posteriori* basis; it takes for granted what it cannot prove, namely, the trustworthiness of sense perception, and thus it is vulnerable to skeptical challenges. Only philosophical reasoning can establish the foundations of science by somehow justifying

8. For an exposition and critique of modern scientism, see J. P. Moreland, *Scientism and Secularism* (Wheaton, IL: Crossway, 2018).

9. W. V. Quine, "Epistemology Naturalized," in *Ontological Relativity and Other Essays* (New York: Columbia University Press, 1969), 69–90.

a priori our assumption that sense experience gives us reliable access to an orderly external world that exists independently of our minds. Yet this foundationalist project, epitomized by the "first philosophy" of René Descartes, has faltered—or so Quine contended. Hume argued that reason is unable to underwrite our ideas about an external world and to justify our inductive inferences about general laws of nature that enable us to predict future events. No philosopher who is committed to Hume's naturalistic approach has been able to solve the problems exposed by Hume. Thus, Quine lamented, "the Humean predicament is the human predicament."

The only recourse, according to Quine, is to abandon as futile the project of traditional epistemology. Rather than viewing epistemology as a normative discipline that establishes *a priori* principles for underwriting science, it should instead be viewed as a naturalistic discipline that contents itself with describing how people actually think and reason about the world. On this view, science doesn't need to be justified by philosophy. We simply take it as it is, and that frees us to use science to answer the only questions that epistemologists really need to ask. Quine is clear, however, that this demands a radical reconstruction of the project of epistemology: "Epistemology, or something like it, simply falls into place as a chapter of psychology and hence of natural science. It studies a natural phenomenon, viz., a physical human subject."[10] Such words would surely have been music to Hume's ears.

The question of whether epistemology should be naturalized (and, if so, to what extent) has become one of the major debates in contemporary philosophy. Advocates of traditional epistemology have criticized the movement on several fronts: it dodges the age-old challenge of skepticism, it embraces a vicious circularity

10. Ibid., 82.

by employing empirical psychology to answer "epistemological" (i.e., psychological) questions, and it is guilty of simply changing the subject by abandoning the normative questions of epistemology ("What beliefs *should* we hold?"). The basic problem, the critics complain, is that "naturalized epistemology" isn't really epistemology at all. Whatever course this debate takes, one thing is clear: the naturalization project is Humean through and through.

The Evidentialist Challenge

It is fair to say that skepticism reigns in the Western world with respect to religious claims. The received wisdom among the intelligentsia is that natural theology never recovered from its pummeling at the hands of Hume and Kant. Even those who hold strong religious convictions are prone to confess that their convictions are held "by faith, not by reason."

In addition to his critique of the traditional theistic proofs, Hume's argument against miracles continues to exert its influence on modern skeptics. To take one example: in his popular book *Jesus, Interrupted*, Bart Ehrman argues that a scholarly, historical approach to the Gospels requires us to reject the many miracle stories they contain. It is not simply that there is insufficient evidence for miracles; rather, as a matter of principle, there cannot be historical evidence for a miracle.[11] As Ehrman explains,

> All that historians can do is show what probably happened in the past. That is the problem with miracles. Miracles, by our very definition of the term, are virtually impossible events. . . . By now I hope you can see the unavoidable problem historians have with miracles. Historians can only establish what

11. Bart D. Ehrman, *Jesus, Interrupted* (New York: HarperCollins, 2009), 173.

happened in the past, but miracles, by their very nature, are always the least probable explanation for what happened.[12]

Ehrman's debt to Hume, though wholly unacknowledged, should be obvious.[13]

Hume is arguably the fountainhead of a more general criticism of religious beliefs, which we might call the *evidentialist challenge*. Recall his dictum: "A wise man proportions his belief to the evidence." The insinuation is unmistakable: religious claims typically lack the kind of evidence that would justify our believing them. In his essay "The Ethics of Belief," the philosopher William Clifford offered a more vigorous formulation of Hume's principle: "It is wrong always, everywhere, and for anyone, to believe anything upon insufficient evidence."[14] Similar evidentialist sentiments lie behind Carl Sagan's popularization of the maxim "Extraordinary claims require extraordinary evidence"—a slogan never far from the keyboards of the self-styled freethinking skeptics who populate Internet debate forums.

The evidentialist challenge to Christianity can be concisely stated as a simple syllogism:

Premise 1: A belief is rationally justified only if it is supported by sufficient evidence.

Premise 2: Christian beliefs are not supported by sufficient evidence.

12. Ibid., 175.
13. In May 2018, Sam Harris's *Waking Up* podcast featured a conversation with Ehrman. Right on cue, as the discussion turned to the topic of Christ's resurrection, Harris cited Hume's argument against reported miracles. See https://samharris.org /podcasts/what-is-christianity/.
14. W. K. Clifford, "The Ethics of Belief," *Contemporary Review* 29 (1876–77): 289–309.

Conclusion: Christian beliefs are not rationally justified.

Christian apologists in the evidentialist tradition have generally directed their firepower at refuting Premise 2, and on the face of it that seems like the most appealing strategy. Who wouldn't want to say that their beliefs are supported by good evidence?

There are, however, two other important responses to the evidentialist challenge, which we will consider in more detail in chapters 7 and 8: Alvin Plantinga's Reformed epistemology, which challenges Premise 1, and Cornelius Van Til's transcendental presuppositionalism, which simultaneously challenges both premises. Suffice it to say for now that the landscape of contemporary Christian apologetics has largely been formed in response to the evidentialist challenge of Hume and his heirs.

6

A REFORMED ASSESSMENT
OF HUME'S THOUGHT

This chapter marks a shift of gears from exposition to evaluation. Having summarized Hume's philosophical project, his naturalistic approach to ethics, and his skeptical stance toward religion, we will enter into a critical assessment of his thought from a distinctively Reformed perspective, generally following the presuppositional approach pioneered by Cornelius Van Til. This critical assessment will consist of four basic elements:

1. We will note how Hume's presuppositions—his foundational assumptions and his philosophical method—are at odds with a Reformed Christian worldview.
2. We will consider how Hume's deviation from a Reformed Christian worldview leads to various problematic implications and ultimately to self-defeating skepticism.
3. We will identify several internal flaws in Hume's philosophy, demonstrating how it fails even on its own terms.
4. We will respond to Hume's various objections to the

Christian religion, noting how his criticisms are founded on disputable and question-begging assumptions.

In what follows, the phrase "Reformed Christian worldview" will be used as shorthand for the theological and philosophical outlook reflected in the historic Reformed creeds and confessions, the distinctive tenets of which would include:

- The triune God as the absolutely sovereign and self-contained creator, sustainer, and governor of all things other than God.
- The creation of man in the image of God, the highest end of man being to glorify and delight in God.
- The historical fall of man into sin, the subsequent corruption of the created order, and the debilitating effects of sin on every human faculty (the doctrines traditionally known as original sin and total depravity).
- The clear, sufficient, and authoritative self-revelation of God in nature and Scripture.
- A philosophy of history centered on the outworking of God's redemptive plan, first in the history of Israel and then in the history of the church.
- The incarnation, atonement, resurrection, ascension, and intercession of Jesus Christ, the Son of God, the only mediator between God and man.
- The outpouring of the Holy Spirit at Pentecost and his ongoing application of the redemptive work of Christ to the church.
- The salvation of sinners by grace alone through faith alone in Christ alone, with all glory given to God alone.
- An eschatological hope focused on the final resurrection and judgment, followed by the re-creation and restoration of the cosmos.

Perhaps to some readers it will seem objectionably prejudicial and question-begging to presuppose a Reformed Christian worldview in our assessment of Hume's thought. But no critique can proceed from a presuppositional vacuum; there can be no leverage without a fulcrum. As we have already noted, Hume's critique of the Christian faith is founded on substantive philosophical (and implicitly theological) assumptions. What's sauce for the goose is sauce for the gander.[1]

Our evaluation of Hume's thought will begin in this chapter with a general critique of his philosophical project, focusing on problems with his empiricist epistemology and his naturalistic ethics. Chapter 7 will offer a Reformed response to Hume's religious skepticism. Chapter 8 will demonstrate how Hume's work, despite his intentions, provides useful material for Christian apologetics.

Was Hume a Great Thinker?

Before embarking further, there is one important question we ought to address. Was David Hume a great thinker? On what grounds does he merit inclusion in a "Great Thinkers" series?

If the criterion for judging someone to be a great thinker is the extent of his influence on subsequent thinkers, Hume's credentials have already been established. But sheer influence cannot be the sole criterion. No doubt Muhammad's teachings had tremendous influence on such medieval philosophers as Averröes and Al-Ghazali, but it would be a stretch to claim that Muhammad himself was a great thinker.

Hume was no friend of the Christian faith. Nevertheless,

---

1. For a further defense of this stance, see James N. Anderson, "Presuppositionalism and Frame's Epistemology," in *Speaking the Truth in Love: The Theology of John M. Frame*, ed. John J. Hughes (Phillipsburg, NJ: P&R Publishing, 2009), 431–59, particularly the section "Divine Lordship: Presuppositionalism in Principle."

there are still several respects in which Christians can give him credit and even admire aspects of his thought. In the first place, we can appreciate the comprehensive sweep of his philosophical project: nothing short of a "complete science of human nature," based solely on the "experimental method." Hume's project is highly ambitious, yet also well-defined, focused, and methodical. His fundamental division of perceptions (i.e., experiences) into impressions and ideas, combined with the Copy Principle that sovereignly governs his analyses of various topics, presents an appealingly simple foundation for a philosophical system.

Furthermore, Hume adopts a "from square one" approach to the objects of his inquiries. While he acknowledges previous thinkers, Hume never adopts their views merely on authority, but rather seeks to defend (or refute) those ideas on his own terms, in accordance with the first principles he believes he has established. His methodology is strict and unforgiving: if an idea cannot be justified on the basis of reason or experience, it should be discarded, no matter what the source of that idea may be.

Although there are some blind spots in Hume's thought, as we will see shortly, his desire for systematic consistency is hard to fault. Even when he recognizes the counterintuitive or disconcerting implications of his views, he doesn't shrink back from drawing those conclusions. His logical incisiveness and intellectual honesty are refreshing, even when it takes him far from what Christians would regard as a healthy view of the world. The Reformed apologist Cornelius Van Til notes that

> the non-Christian may have, and often does have, a brilliant mind. It may act efficiently, like a sharp circular saw acts efficiently.[2]

2. Cornelius Van Til, *The Defense of the Faith*, ed. K. Scott Oliphint, 4th ed. (Phillipsburg, NJ: P&R Publishing, 2008), 293.

Yet the saw's blade is out of kilter. It may cut straight and deep, but the wood is "cut slantwise and thus unusable."[3] Van Til's metaphor fits Hume to a tee.

Finally, it is fair to say that Hume's thought encapsulates, more strikingly than that of any of his contemporaries, the spirit of the Enlightenment: human reason and experience as the final judges of what is true and right, the scientific method as normative for human knowledge, and mounting skepticism about traditional religious claims. Even today, thinkers who grapple with the major questions of metaphysics, epistemology, ethics, and the philosophy of science, largely follow an agenda set by Hume. The problems he identified and the solutions he offered continue to play a central role in philosophical discussions.

The Presumption of Naturalism

Hume's *presumptive naturalism* is arguably the one point at which his worldview differs most foundationally from that of biblical Christianity. His stated goal was to develop a comprehensive account of human thought and action that would be no less scientific than Newtonian physics. Humans are assumed to be entirely part of the natural order, governed by relatively simple laws of cause and effect, and thus explicable in terms of such laws. This is not to say that Hume is committed to materialism; that would be too dogmatically metaphysical. Although he thinks no one can really take Berkeley's idealism seriously, neither can it be refuted by reason or experience (*THN* 1.4.2).[4] So Hume's presumption isn't metaphysical, so much as methodological;

---

3. Ibid., 97.

4. George Berkeley (1685–1753) was an Irish philosopher and Anglican bishop who argued against the existence of mind-independent material substances and defended metaphysical idealism (the theory that only minds and ideas really exist). He is best known for his maxim *esse est percipi* (to be is to be perceived).

it limits the kind of descriptions and explanations that he will accept in his "science" of human nature. Certainly any references to unobserved (and unobservable) entities, such as God, angels, spirits, and souls, are off the table.

Hume's naturalism is not held tentatively as a kind of working hypothesis that could be proven false in the course of his explorations. It is evident from all his writings, from the *Treatise* to the *Dialogues*, that his naturalism functions as a nonnegotiable axiom. Given his starting assumptions, there is no evidence in principle that could establish the existence of nonnatural entities or supernatural causes. Even when he concedes (somewhat reluctantly) that there probably exists some intelligent cause behind the universe, it is clear that whatever that cause might be, it would be of the same order as the universe itself. It couldn't be a fundamentally different kind of being, such as the God of classical Christian theism. It would merely be one being among others, rather than Being itself. In the end, the only gods Hume countenances are gods of nature: natural extensions of the space-time cosmos.

This observation has two significant implications. First, it means that Hume essentially begs the question against the Christian from the outset. God isn't so much refuted as precluded. Any elements of the Christian faith that cannot be explicated in naturalistic terms must be dismissed or denied as a point of principle. Yet one searches Hume's works in vain for a principled argument for his naturalistic presuppositions. They are, in effect, an article of faith. But if Hume can take empirical naturalism on faith, then the Christian is entirely within his rights to take biblical supernaturalism on faith and to develop an account of human nature on those terms.

Second, Hume's presumptive naturalism means that his net will only catch certain fish. Given the constraints of his starting point and method, it is impossible for him to reach certain kinds of conclusions or to countenance certain kinds of explanations. Moreover, these constraints are suspiciously restrictive and artificial. Why the presumption of naturalism? Why restrict one's options so prejudicially? It is as though Hume sets out to paint the world, but determines at the outset to paint solely in shades of gray. If the world is in fact entirely gray, all well and good. But what if the world is multicolored? Hume's naturalistic palette cannot hope to capture it accurately.

The Presumption of Autonomy

From a Reformed Christian perspective, another fatal problem with Hume's philosophical project is that it presumes the *autonomy* of the human mind. Hume takes for granted that our intellectual faculties—specifically, reason and experience—are competent in themselves to make judgments about what is true and right. Indeed, his position is that reason and experience must be the ultimate authorities regarding what we should believe and how we should act. Our faculties are assumed to be self-justifying and independent of any external authorities, such as the mind of God or divine revelation.

One might respond that Hume means only to minimize his starting assumptions, to assume no more than he must assume in order to get his project off the ground. Don't we all have to take for granted that our reason and experience are basically trustworthy guides to truth? Indeed we do, but there is a significant difference between taking reason and experience as proximate starting points for knowledge and treating them as ultimate criteria for knowledge. The first is consistent with a Reformed Christian worldview; the second is not.

Furthermore, if one begins by assuming the authority of human reason and the competence of the human mind without also acknowledging our absolute dependence on God, that is tantamount to denying that the God of the Bible exists, because it assumes (contrary to a biblical worldview) that human reason can operate independently of God and his self-revelation. It assumes that we can, at least in principle, acquire knowledge of ourselves and the world regardless of whether God exists. But once that stance is adopted, it becomes impossible to countenance the existence of the true God. Any deity that autonomous reason and experience could disclose to us would fall short of the absolute, sovereign Lord of Scripture. To put the matter somewhat differently: one cannot accept the lordship of Christ over the entire sphere of human thought and action while also assuming the autonomy of the human mind.[5]

We can thus see how Hume begs the question against the Reformed Christian in a second respect. The starting point for his philosophical project is such that it excludes biblical theism from the very outset. Consequently, it comes as no surprise when he concludes that the claims of Christianity cannot be established by reason or experience. The deck has been stacked. The dice have been weighted.

Hume's presumption of naturalism is closely allied with his presumption of autonomy. Given naturalism, there can be no transcendent God who intervenes in the natural world and speaks with authority to us; thus, it makes no sense to say that our minds are subject to the authority of a higher divine mind. Conversely, if we assume at the outset that our intellectual faculties are self-justifying and independent of any external authority, we thereby exclude the existence of any God worthy of that title, and epistemological atheism becomes the doorway to methodological naturalism. As I will argue later, however, Hume's twin presumptions spell doom for his entire project because they

5. One thinks of Abraham Kuyper's famous declaration: "There is not a square inch in the whole domain of our human existence over which Christ, who is Sovereign over all, does not cry: 'Mine!'"

open the door to a debilitating skepticism that runs even deeper than Hume concedes.

Internal Problems

Let us turn now to consider some internal problems with Hume's project, beginning with his theory of the mind, which is foundational to his entire science of human nature.

Recall that Hume refers to all mental content as *perceptions* and posits a basic division between *ideas* and *impressions*. Although this division is treated like a categorical distinction, as though there were something essentially different between ideas and impressions, this is not how Hume actually draws the distinction. Rather, the distinction is one of degree, rather than kind: impressions differ from ideas in "the degrees of force and liveliness" (*THN* 1.1.1.1). Hume seems to assume that there is some threshold of forcefulness above which a perception must be regarded as an impression, rather than as an idea. In most cases, impressions and ideas are "easily distinguished," although he grants that sometimes they may "very nearly approach to each other," as though there were some kind of mental no-man's-land between the realm of ideas and the realm of impressions. The problem is that by Hume's own lights this isn't something he could know *a priori*, and thus there is no reason to rule out a continuum of perceptions of differing degrees of liveliness. As such, Hume ought to speak only of weaker and stronger perceptions or ideas.[6]

The illusion that there is a categorical difference between impressions and ideas is subtly reinforced by the terminology that Hume adopts. By definition, an impression is the result of one thing impressing upon another thing. It is an inherently

---

6. Hume's suggestion that the distinction between impressions and ideas amounts to "the difference betwixt feeling and thinking" is merely a restatement, rather than an elucidation, of the distinction.

causal notion. Thus, by speaking of impressions, Hume gives the impression (pun intended) that our mental perception of a tree is caused by some object external to the mind. Yet this is wholly inconsistent with what Hume insists elsewhere, namely, that we cannot know causation *a priori* and that there is no rational basis for believing in an external mind-independent world. The most basic distinction in Hume's theory of the mind seems to presuppose concepts that his theory eventually rejects.

The irony should not be missed. At the very outset, Hume makes subtle assumptions that he would have dismissed as unjustified and even unintelligible, had he identified them in other philosophers. Once we strip away those assumptions, Hume's theory of the mind reduces to this: we just happen to have a series of perceptions with varying degrees of force and liveliness. Nothing whatever can be assumed—or concluded—about the sources or causes of these perceptions.

This in turn introduces difficulties for Hume's Copy Principle, which depends crucially on the distinction between impressions and ideas. In light of the above, the Copy Principle should be revised along these lines:

> All our simple *perceptions of lesser force* in their first appearance are derived from simple *perceptions of greater force*, which are correspondent to them, and which they exactly represent.

The trouble is that this proposition is catastrophically vague and unable to do the heavy lifting that Hume wants it to do. Without a categorical distinction between different kinds of perceptions, the Copy Principle is practically worthless.

Even if we disregard these problems, there is a further difficulty with Hume's theory of the mind. Let us grant, for the sake of argument, Hume's distinction between impressions and ideas. As Hume sees matters, all simple ideas are representations (that is, faint copies) of prior simple impressions, and all simple impressions have a *sensational* quality to them: the redness of a tomato, the smoothness of the table, the pleasantness of your friend's virtues, and so on. They are *feelings*, rather than *thoughts* (*THN* 1.1.1.1). On this view, all perceptions must be understood as mental images: not necessarily visual images, but nonetheless possessing ordinary sensible qualities or some analogue of such qualities.

This invites an obvious objection: we seem to be able to entertain many ideas—perfectly intelligible ones—that simply could not be traced back to simple impressions because they lack any sensible qualities or features. Take, for example, our idea of the number two. Clearly that's an intelligible concept. (The fact that you understood the previous two sentences proves the point.) Yet that idea cannot be traced back to any original impressions of which it is a representation. No doubt we often have impressions of two concrete things (e.g., two chairs), but that's not at all the same as having an impression of the number two as such. Two chairs have size, color, texture, and so forth. The number two has none of those features. It is an abstract mathematical object.[7]

Such examples can be multiplied. Consider a concept that has become important in modern science: the idea of a quark (a type of elementary particle). Physical objects are made up of quarks, and physical objects have sensible qualities, but quarks themselves do not. No one has a mental image of a quark. On Hume's view, we shouldn't be able to have the idea of a quark—but tens of thousands of particle physicists would beg to differ. Although he considered it supremely scientific, Hume's theory of the mind would spell disaster for modern science.

Indeed, things may be even worse for Hume because his

---

7. Here we need to resist the modern materialistic prejudice that all objects of thought must be material or sensible in nature. We should also avoid confusing numbers with numerals (the symbols we use to denote numbers).

theory appears to be self-defeating. Consider the idea of a perception (i.e., Hume's most basic unit of mental content). Hume's theory depends on that idea being intelligible, but what specific impressions could give rise to that abstract idea? Can you trace your *idea* of an impression back to one or more original impressions? What could those impressions possibly be?

Hume's root error is that he formulates his theory of the mind from the wrong end. Rather than starting with the various intelligible (and in some cases indispensable) ideas that we do in fact possess, and then reasoning about the possible sources of those ideas, he starts instead with an artificially restrictive view of the origin of our ideas and is subsequently committed to various counterintuitive (and in some cases self-defeating) conclusions about which ideas we can cognitively entertain.

Similar problems afflict his empiricist epistemology. According to Hume, the faculty of reason can deliver only two kinds of beliefs: relations of ideas (i.e., logical or definitional truths, such as "All cats are animals") and matters of fact (i.e., contingent truths about the world, such as "The cat is on the mat"). Thus, given Hume's position, only beliefs about conceptual truths and about empirical facts can be rationally justified. Several serious problems afflict this restrictive position. In the first place, there are countless beliefs that we ordinarily take to be rationally justified, but which do not correspond to either prong of Hume's Fork. Consider these examples:

- The angles of a triangle add up to 180 degrees.
- Water is H_2O.
- No object is entirely red and entirely blue at the same time.
- It is morally wrong to torture children for entertainment.

I would imagine that most readers would say that we know these propositions to be true. At a minimum, we are rationally justified in believing all four propositions. Yet none of these propositions are strictly logical truths; none can be deduced merely from the laws of logic or from the definitions of the words used. Furthermore, each proposition is plausibly a *necessary* truth that could not be (or have been) false, which means that none of them meet Hume's definition of a matter of fact. (For Hume, a matter of fact is always a *contingent* truth.)

In addition, there are contingent truths that are entirely rational to believe, but which cannot be known by empirical observation alone, such as:

- There exist minds other than our own.
- The universe exists independently of our experiences of it.
- The universe has existed for more than a week.
- Our sensory faculties are generally reliable.

The problem, once again, is that Hume approaches epistemological questions from the wrong end. He begins with an artificially restrictive criterion for knowledge and then implausibly rules out various commonsense beliefs as rationally unsupportable, when he ought to begin by surveying the beliefs that we generally take to be rationally justified before asking what features they have in common.

A defender of Hume might object that this begs the question by simply assuming we are rationally justified in believing the sort of propositions I've suggested here. But this isn't mere assumption; it is based on widely held intuitive convictions. Sound philosophy ought to explain our pre-philosophical intuitions, rather than (as Hume does) trying to explain them away. In reality, Hume himself begs the question by simply assuming his two-pronged criterion for rational beliefs. Indeed, not only is his criterion unjustified, it is self-defeating. Consider the following formulation of Hume's Fork:

(HF) A belief can be rationally justified only if it concerns relations of ideas or matters of fact.

Presumably Hume believed HF to be true. But does HF itself concern relations of ideas or matters of fact? No, it doesn't: it is neither true by definition nor grounded in sense experience. If HF were true, it would be a synthetic *a priori* truth—precisely the kind of truth that Hume deems to be beyond the grasp of reason. Thus, if Hume's Fork is true, it cannot be rationally justified.

Finally, we should not overlook a serious internal problem with Hume's account of causation. Recall that, according to Hume, our concept of causation includes the idea of *necessary connection*, but neither reason nor experience can actually establish any objectively necessary connection between events. Instead, we observe only the *constant conjunction* of pairs of events, and over the course of time, by a natural psychological process, we come to habitually expect one type of event to follow another. In other words, whenever we observe (or merely contemplate) the first type of event, our minds will naturally form a belief that the second type of event will follow it. But these beliefs about cause and effect are the fruit of custom rather than reason.

The elementary flaw in this account of causal beliefs is that it turns out to be circular, since it presupposes causal relations. Habit is an inherently causal notion: it implies that a cause (in this case, a constant conjunction of perceptions) brings about a specific effect (in this case, beliefs about necessary connections). But Hume has no right to appeal to a causal process in his account of causation, given the restrictions he imposes on that account. The most he is permitted to say is that we observe a constant conjunction between (1) our observations of constant conjunctions and (2) our beliefs about necessary connections (i.e., causal relations). Given Hume's own terms, there is no reason to expect that we will always expect certain events to follow other events. Hume's psychological account of causation turns out to be self-defeating. Either it must assume what it denies (objective necessary connections) or it sinks into an ocean of pure subjectivity.

The Specter of Solipsism

There is one further objection to Hume's philosophical project that is worth highlighting. Hume boasts that his complete science of human nature will rest entirely on the "experimental method," which means that his claims about human thoughts and actions will be grounded in ideas traceable entirely to original sensory impressions.

But *whose* impressions?

For Hume, the answer must be: Hume's impressions—and no others. All of Hume's conclusions must, by his own lights, derive entirely from his own ideas and impressions—the perceptions that arise within his own mind—because he has no epistemic access to anything else. And, as he himself argues, he has no rational basis for believing in an external mind-independent world, the existence of other minds, or even the existence of a unified self that persists through time.

Thus, the specter of solipsism looms large for Hume, and he has no power to banish it. One who follows Hume must be willing to accept that there is no reason to believe that anything is real beyond one's own ideas and impressions. A faithful Humean will insist that nature prevents us from embracing solipsism. We are psychologically unable to believe such an absurdity! But such a response misses the point: it still gives us no *reason* to reject solipsism. Worse still, it begs the question, for the very notion of "nature" presupposes that solipsism is false.

This crippling problem for Hume can be posed in the form of a dilemma. He wants to make general claims about how *humans* think and act, not merely about how *Hume* thinks and acts. But his strict empiricism and his restrictive theory of the mind make it impossible for him to reach beyond the latter. Hume has no basis for extrapolating from his own mind to other minds. There seem to be only two escape routes available: abandon his empiricism or retreat into solipsism. Neither route is Hume willing to take.

A Matter of Taste

Our assessment of Hume's general project would be incomplete without some consideration of his moral theory. Space constraints forbid an extended critique, so we will confine ourselves to three critical observations about Hume's naturalistic account of ethics, focusing on some foundational difficulties with that account.

Recall that Hume's approach is a combination of *moral sentimentalism* and *virtue ethics*. The core idea is simple enough: whenever we perceive certain character traits in others or ourselves, we experience feelings of pleasure or displeasure. For Hume, this is part of our natural disposition and can be established by observation. Virtues are understood to be those traits we approve, while vices are those we disapprove. On this account, moral qualities are not objective features of the world (and thus not objective features of humans themselves), but rather are secondary qualities that exist only as effects within the mind. Hume explicitly draws a parallel between our perceptions of moral qualities and our perceptions of sounds, colors, temperatures, and other secondary qualities (*THN* 3.1.1.26).

We noted earlier that Hume's account has often been characterized as noncognitivist and criticized for that reason. On his view, so it is argued, there are no moral truths—an implication that is highly counterintuitive, if not altogether absurd. But this isn't wholly fair, for Hume believes that we can make meaningful moral judgments that are true or false, just as we can make meaningful statements about the color of the sky or the warmth of our coffee. Nevertheless, there is a closely related objection to be raised here. Hume maintains that moral qualities are subjective and contingent, from which two things follow: they don't have to be universal across the human race, and they could have been different than they actually are.

To see the problem, consider a parallel case: the color spectrum. When you perceive a red object, you have a different subjective experience than when you perceive a blue object. Put simply, red looks different than blue. Physicists tell us that red objects have different physical properties than blue objects (i.e., they reflect different frequencies of light waves), and we assume that there is a causal connection between the objective physical properties and our subjective perceptions. We also take for granted that people have basically the same subjective perceptions. Those who are able to perceive red and blue experience them in much the same way.

There is, however, no necessary connection between the objective physical properties and our subjective perceptions. In theory, our experiences of colors could have been different. There is a possible world in which the color of the sky is experienced exactly as we now experience red objects.[8] If this is true for colors, then on Hume's view it must be equally true for virtues and vices. Our experiences of pleasure and displeasure at certain character traits could have been different. Indeed, our "moral

8. Hume's predecessor, John Locke, was one of the first philosophers to reflect on the possibility of an "inverted spectrum" of color perception. Some have argued that this isn't a real possibility, but for Hume whatever is conceivable without contradiction is possible (and there is no contradiction in the idea of an inverted spectrum).

spectrum" could have been completely inverted, such that what we regard as virtues would have been vices—and vice versa (so to speak). Loyalty could have been morally bad, and disloyalty morally good.[9] Such a counterintuitive implication suggests a fundamental flaw in Hume's theory.

The upshot of Hume's account is that ethics, like aesthetics, is reduced to matters of personal taste. Hume may wish to speak of moral tastes, distinct from other kinds of tastes, and he can argue that there is (as a matter of empirical fact) a consensus about morals, just as there can be a consensus about what constitutes beautiful art or fine wine, but the point remains: Humean discourse on morals is nothing more than a way of speaking about arbitrary subjective experiences. One of the central concerns of metaethics is to account for the normativity of morality. Hume seeks to ground that normativity in human sentiments alone, with the inevitable consequence that moral norms become entirely subjective and contingent.[10]

This prompts a second line of objection. For Hume, a moral virtue is by definition a trait for which we feel approval, a trait that gives us pleasure. But this seems obviously mistaken, for there is nothing incoherent about the idea of a morally bad pleasure. Isn't it at least possible for one to experience pleasure at someone else's (or their own) immoral behavior or corrupt character? If such a scenario is conceivable without contradiction, then by Hume's lights it must be possible. But in that case

---

9. Alternatively, imagine a situation in which the entire human race contracts a virulent neurological disease, one effect of which is to reverse our moral sentiments. Hume would have to grant the possibility of such a scenario. On Hume's theory, the outbreak would entail the reversal of all moral truths. Dishonesty would literally become virtuous, and so on.

10. In one essay, Hume explicitly denies objective normativity, insisting that all values are grounded in human sentiments: "Objects have absolutely no worth or value in themselves. They derive their worth merely from the passion" (David Hume, "The Sceptic," essay 9 in *Essays, Moral and Political*, vol. 2 [1742]).

Hume's definitions of virtue and vice come apart at the seams. If there can be such a thing as a morally bad pleasure, it follows that morality has to be defined independently of our subjective experiences.

Thirdly, we may observe that Hume provides no satisfactory account of moral obligations or duties, which are integral components of our commonsense understanding of morality. We generally take for granted that we have obligations to each another. For example, if I make a promise to you, I have a duty to keep that promise—or at least a duty to try to keep it to the best of my ability, barring exceptional circumstances. My act of promising incurs a kind of moral debt that needs to be satisfied: I *owe* it to you to keep my promise. This moral obligation cannot be reduced to mere subjective perceptions. It is a real objective constraint that exists between us, regardless of anyone's feelings or experiences.

Nothing in Hume's theory of moral sentiments begins to explain how there can be real moral obligations that obtain between human beings. At most, his psychological account could explain why we *feel* a sense of moral duty. But that does not at all explain how there could be moral duties in any objective sense, any more than Hume's psychological account of causation provides grounds for thinking that there are real objective causal relations.[11]

From a Christian perspective, moral obligations need to be grounded in an appropriate moral authority, and absolute moral obligations—duties that apply to all people in all circumstances, irrespective of their feelings and experiences—need to be

---

11. To be fair, Hume believes that he has provided an account of moral obligations, but what he really offers (as with his account of causation) is a revisionist theory in which such obligations are reconceived as merely psychological (see, e.g., *THN* 3.2.5). That is why I say that he provides no satisfactory account. One does not adequately explain X by denying X and explaining Y instead.

grounded in an absolute moral authority. As a naturalist, Hume cannot appeal to God as the source of moral obligations. But there is no substitute for God in his system. Unable to explain our moral obligations on a naturalistic basis, Hume essentially explains them away.[12]

---

12. This last point of critique could be reformulated in terms of universal human rights. On a Humean view, there can be no such thing—at least, not in any literal sense.

7

A REFORMED RESPONSE TO HUME'S RELIGIOUS SKEPTICISM

Bertrand Russell, despite his sympathies for Hume's empirical methodology, lamented that Hume's philosophy represents "the bankruptcy of eighteenth-century reasonableness," a "dead end" beyond which "it is impossible to go further."[1] In light of the previous chapter, it is hard to disagree with Russell's verdict. Even so, the fact that Hume's own system of thought is hopeless doesn't automatically nullify his critique of religion. For this reason, and because Hume-inspired objections continue to be wielded by skeptics in our day, we must explore a Reformed response to the three main aspects of Hume's critique: the evidentialist challenge, his argument against miracles, and his attempted debunking of natural theology.

1. Bertrand Russell, *A History of Western Philosophy* (New York: Simon & Schuster, 1945), 672, 659.

Defusing the Evidentialist Challenge

In chapter 5, we noted that Hume is one of the major influences behind the evidentialist challenge to Christian beliefs, which we summarized as a simple syllogism:

Premise 1: A belief is rationally justified only if it is supported by sufficient evidence.

Premise 2: Christian beliefs are not supported by sufficient evidence.

Conclusion: Christian beliefs are not rationally justified.

Christian apologists operating within the evidentialist tradition, such as Joseph Butler (1692–1752), William Paley (1743–1805), and more recently Richard Swinburne, have tended to focus on rebutting Premise 2. This strategy is entirely understandable and can be quite effective in practice. This is not the place to review evidential arguments for Christian claims; here I will simply note that advances in scientific understanding and historical research since Hume's day have served only to fortify the evidential support for the central tenets of Christianity.

That said, we should recognize that Premise 1 of the challenge is no less disputable. Recall the frequently quoted maxim from Hume's first *Enquiry*: "A wise man proportions his belief to the evidence." It shouldn't escape notice that Hume himself did not—and could not—follow his own maxim consistently. He undoubtedly believed that other minds than his own existed, that his impressions were caused by an external world, that objects continue to exist when unperceived, and that the sun would rise every morning. By his own standards of evidence (i.e., what can be established by reason and sense experience alone), none of these beliefs enjoyed any evidential support whatever.

Hume's response, of course, would be to concede that none of these beliefs are rationally justified, but to insist that we are nevertheless naturally disposed to hold them. Nature compels us to believe those things; we have no choice in the matter.[2] There are two problems with this response. First, if nature compels us to believe certain things, then Hume's maxim makes no sense. It is futile to instruct a man to proportion his belief to the evidence, if he cannot believe otherwise. Second, if it is acceptable to hold some nonreligious metaphysical beliefs without rational justification, why wouldn't it be equally acceptable to hold some religious metaphysical beliefs without rational justification? Perhaps nature compels some people to believe in the existence of an all-good, all-powerful God!

Let us refocus on Premise 1 of the evidentialist challenge. One good reason to reject this proposition is that it appears to be self-defeating. If Premise 1 is true, then we should believe it only if it is supported by sufficient evidence. But is it? What kind of evidence do we have to support Premise 1? Certainly no evidence of the kind accepted by Hume could justify it, for it isn't a deliverance of pure reason or an empirically observable matter of fact. So why should a Humean believe Premise 1?

A further problem with Premise 1 is that it fails to account for the prevalence of properly basic beliefs.[3] A properly basic belief is a belief that is rationally justified (i.e., we are within our "epistemic rights" to hold it), even though it isn't derived or inferred from other rationally justified beliefs. It turns out that a significant proportion of the everyday beliefs we hold are properly basic: beliefs based on sense perception; beliefs produced by our

2. See, e.g., *THN* 1.4.1.7, 1.4.2.1, 1.4.2.51–52.
3. See Alvin Plantinga, "Is Belief in God Properly Basic?," *Nous* 15 (1981): 41–51.

memories; beliefs about foundational logical, mathematical, and moral principles; beliefs based on testimony; and so on. When we examine these beliefs, it is clear that we don't hold them on the basis of evidence—at least, not the kind of evidence that those who press the evidentialist challenge have in mind. Indeed, in many cases it is unclear what kind of evidence one could have for such beliefs. (For example, what evidence would you cite in support of your belief that you are not inside the Matrix?) Yet it would be perverse to require people to relinquish all these properly basic beliefs.

This observation about properly basic beliefs helped to inspire the Reformed epistemology movement led by such Christian philosophers as Alvin Plantinga, Nicholas Wolterstorff, and William Alston. One of the central claims of Reformed epistemology is that belief in God can be (and typically is) properly basic, in much the same way that beliefs about other minds, the external world, the reliability of our senses, the uniformity of nature, and so forth, are properly basic. Drawing from the writings of John Calvin and the Reformed tradition, Plantinga has argued forcefully that if a personal Creator exists, then it is very likely that humans possess a cognitive faculty—a *sensus divinitatis*—that is designed by that Creator to deliver true beliefs about him. Such beliefs would not be inferential in nature, deriving their rational justification from philosophical arguments or empirical evidences, as traditional natural theology seeks to do. Instead, they would be formed non-inferentially and would be justified merely by virtue of being produced by a properly functioning cognitive faculty (as is the case for beliefs formed directly by our other cognitive faculties, such as memory and sense perception). On this view, theistic beliefs would be both natural and rational. Indeed, in his magnum opus, *Warranted Christian Belief*, Plantinga goes on to argue that not only theistic beliefs, but also distinctively Christian beliefs (e.g., that Jesus is the Son of God and that the Bible is the Word of God) can be properly basic, since they are produced directly by the internal witness of the Holy Spirit on the basis of the divine testimony of Scripture.[4]

Whether Plantinga's theory about Christian beliefs is correct is not the point. The fact is that the kind of scenario proposed by the Reformed epistemologists doesn't seem to have even occurred to Hume. It would be unfair to fault Hume for failing to foresee developments in epistemology two centuries after his death, but it does underscore the shortsightedness of his approach to epistemology in general and to religious epistemology in particular.

The rebuttal from the Reformed epistemologists is impressive, but there is a further and deeper response to the evidentialist challenge that can be made, one inspired by the Reformed presuppositionalism of Cornelius Van Til. While concurring with the foregoing responses that Premises 1 and 2 are highly disputable, the presuppositionalist will press further and argue that the evidentialist challenge as a whole depends on presuppositions that are at odds with the skeptic's worldview (i.e., naturalism). There are various ways to bring out this point, but here is one. Premise 1 takes for granted that we have minds with a faculty of reason that reliably directs us toward truth and that there are objective intellectual norms that govern our thoughts and beliefs. In other words, the evidentialist challenge presupposes that we *ought* to regulate what we believe according to certain rules or standards ("The wise man proportions his belief . . .").

On a naturalistic worldview, however, which holds that human beings (including our minds) are entirely the product of undirected, nonrational, naturalistic processes, there is no basis for such presuppositions. The only objective laws are the laws of nature (although, on Hume's view, even those laws are beyond

---

4. Alvin Plantinga, *Warranted Christian Belief* (Oxford: Oxford University Press, 2000).

the reach of reason). The laws of nature tell us only how nature in fact operates; they have nothing to say about how nature ought to operate. Consequently, the laws of nature cannot ground the kind of intellectual norms that are presupposed by the evidentialist challenge. The very notion of rational justification—an inherently normative concept—makes no sense within a purely naturalistic framework.

In contrast, within a Christian worldview, where human minds derive their purpose and rationality from an Absolute Mind, the idea of intellectual norms makes perfect sense. There is a right way for us to think for the same reason that there is a right way for us to behave: we are creatures made in the image of God, designed to think God's thoughts after him. The evidentialist challenge tacitly presupposes the very worldview it is constructed to refute.

Natural Theology Ex-Humed

"There is no doubt," writes Terence Penelhum, "that Hume's criticisms of natural theology are by far the most substantial in the English language and have been equaled in importance, if at all, only by those of Kant, who was aware of Hume's contributions."[5] Contrast Penelhum's assessment with that of Keith Yandell: "The idea that Hume dealt a deathblow to natural theology is sheer fiction."[6] I submit that both statements are true. Hume's critique of natural theology continues to exert great influence today, even though it falls far short of his ambitions.

Natural theology may be broadly defined as the attempt to

5. Terence Penelhum, "Hume's Criticisms of Natural Theology," in *In Defense of Natural Theology: A Post-Humean Assessment*, ed. James F. Sennett and Douglas Groothuis (Downers Grove, IL: InterVarsity Press, 2005), 40.
6. Keith Yandell, "David Hume on Meaning, Verification and Natural Theology," in *In Defense of Natural Theology*, ed. Sennett and Groothuis, 81.

use natural reason and observation, as opposed to special revelation, to establish truths about the existence and attributes of
God; in other words, it is theology conducted on the basis of natural revelation alone. In the early Enlightenment period, it was
widely assumed that natural theology was necessary for rationally
justified belief in God, and Hume may be forgiven for making
that assumption. In light of the recent work of the Reformed
epistemologists, this can no longer be taken for granted.
Plantinga, Wolterstorff, and others have argued forcefully that
belief in God can be properly basic, being formed directly via
the *sensus divinitatis*. Plantinga has gone so far as to argue that we
can know that the God of the Bible exists without any assistance
from philosophical or evidential arguments. Thus, even if Hume's
objections to the traditional theistic arguments were cogent, it
wouldn't follow that theistic beliefs are epistemically weak.

As it turns out, Hume's critiques are far from cogent, although
here we can only survey some of the main problems. In the
first place, we should note that his critique of natural theology
depends in large measure on his own narrowly empiricist epistemology. Hume divides the theistic arguments into two kinds:
(1) *a priori* deductive proofs, such as the ontological and cosmological arguments, and (2) *a posteriori* analogical arguments
from purpose and order (i.e., teleological arguments). Leaning on
his famous two-pronged fork, Hume holds that *a priori* theistic
proofs must fail because all claims of existence pertain to matters
of fact, yet matters of fact cannot be established on an *a priori*
basis. On the other hand, *a posteriori* arguments from design
inevitably fall short because they seek to draw conclusions that go
far beyond the available observational evidence. If Hume's Fork is
rejected—as it should be, for the reasons already discussed—his
general criticisms of natural theology lose much of their force.

But let us consider his specific objections to the Clarke-style
cosmological argument. Hume maintains that the principle

"Whatever comes into existence must have a cause of its existence" is neither a logical truth (i.e., its denial doesn't involve self-contradiction) nor an empirically established fact. Hume is correct about this, but it doesn't follow that the principle is rationally unjustified. In fact, it is one of many principles that we necessarily take for granted in our reasoning about the world. Indeed, if that principle weren't true, and things can simply pop into existence uncaused, why wouldn't that happen all the time? If a bottle of beer were to inexplicably materialize on the table, it would hardly be reasonable for me to think, "Well, why not?"

Hume also objects to the very idea of necessary existence. His argument is that for any entity X, the nonexistence of X is conceivable without logical contradiction, in which case the nonexistence of X must be possible. The problem here is that Hume fails to recognize the distinction, as philosophers now do, between strict logical possibility and metaphysical possibility. Consider the truth that water is H_2O. That is a matter of fact established by empirical investigation, but it is also a necessary truth about the constitution of water. Water is, in its essence, H_2O. It could not have been anything else, say H_3O, even though we may be able to conceive of that without contradiction. (We can imagine an alternative universe in which scientists analyze the atomic composition of water and it turns out to have *three* hydrogen atoms.) The point is simple: contra Hume, there can be necessary matters of fact.

Furthermore, many philosophers today hold that abstract entities such as numbers and propositions exist necessarily, if they exist at all. There is nothing incoherent about the notion of necessary existence, and there are good reasons to hold that there are some necessary existents. Even so, it is highly implausible to think that the physical universe could be one of them. Every physical object in our experience exists contingently, and the physical universe is just an agglomeration of physical objects.

Hence the Hume-inspired objection, "If something has to exist necessarily, it might as well be the universe," disregards what we already know about the nature of physical objects.

Hume is further mistaken in thinking that if we identify the cause of each individual part of something, we have thereby explained the whole thing itself. A whole is not merely the sum of its parts. There is always a further fact to be explained: how the parts came to constitute the whole. Even if I explain the existence of each individual brick in the wall, I haven't thereby explained the existence of the wall.

In my estimation, Hume's objections to *a priori* theistic arguments are not cogent. His objection to *a posteriori* teleological arguments, however, packs more punch. If such arguments have to be construed as arguments from analogy, it is hard to avoid the conclusion that any intelligent cause behind the universe must be highly anthropomorphic, which is to say, very far from the absolute, transcendent God of the Bible. Likewise, if we are required to argue on a strictly empirical basis, then Hume is correct that the observational data are consistent with multiple hypotheses. Moreover, the mixed moral character of the universe is especially problematic for the hypothesis that the architect of the universe is a perfectly good moral agent.

But once more we find that Hume's analyses are now woefully outdated. Few serious teleological arguments today fit the profile that Hume assumes in the *Dialogues*. The most sophisticated modern design arguments, such as the argument from cosmic fine-tuning and the argument from complex, specified information in biological systems, employ a form of reasoning known as *inference to best explanation*, which incorporates both *a priori* and *a posteriori* considerations to determine whether our overall evidence is best explained on a theistic or a naturalistic basis. The overall evidence will include empirical observations, but can also include rational and moral intuitions. What's more, this holistic approach can show that biblical theism offers a better explanation, all things considered, than competing supernaturalist worldviews such as finite godism or polytheism.

Again, we shouldn't fault Hume for failing to foresee these more sophisticated and powerful forms of argumentation. We should, however, fault those who boast that their champion David felled the Goliath of natural theology once and for all. Anyone who cares to investigate the scholarly literature will discover dozens of contemporary theistic arguments that have been developed in full knowledge of Hume's criticisms and are unscathed by them. Indeed, in the next chapter I will sketch out some arguments, inspired by the presuppositionalism of Cornelius Van Til, that turn Hume's own skeptical philosophy back on itself as an indirect demonstration of God's existence.

Where does all this leave the project of natural theology? Reformed thinkers haven't spoken with one voice on the issue. Some have enthusiastically endorsed the traditional theistic proofs, while others have offered a more qualified affirmation. Still others have rejected natural theology—at least as traditionally conceived—as inconsistent with the Reformed doctrines of God and revelation. The so-called "Reformed objection to natural theology" must be given due consideration.[7] With respect to this in-house debate, one observation will suffice: to the extent that Reformed critics of natural theology rely on Hume's analysis, they lean on a broken reed.

In Defense of Miracles

Hume's "Of Miracles" is still today considered the classic argument against the reasonableness of believing any report of a

7. See Michael Sudduth, *The Reformed Objection to Natural Theology*, Ashgate Philosophy of Religion Series (Burlington, VT: Ashgate, 2009).

miracle. Versions of his argument are regularly wielded by self-styled skeptics and freethinkers against the credibility of the New Testament witness to the miracles of Christ and his apostles. Considerably less well-known today are the various responses to "Of Miracles" by Hume's contemporaries, many of which quite effectively took the wind out of Hume's sails. Especially noteworthy are George Campbell's *A Dissertation on Miracles* (1762) and Richard Price's "On the Importance of Christianity and the Nature of Historical Evidence, and Miracles" (1768), both of which thoroughly dismantle Hume's case against miracles, exposing its many errors of reasoning and misunderstandings of probability theory.

For our purposes, it will suffice to point out the central fallacies in Hume's argument. Some commentators have taken the view that Hume egregiously begs the question by presuming that miracles have in fact never been observed. It is true that some of his statements give this impression. He says, for example, that the laws of nature have been established by "a firm and unalterable experience." If that were so, no future experience could in principle constitute a violation of the laws of nature (or, for that matter, cause us to revise our understanding of the laws of nature). In the same paragraph, Hume remarks that a resurrection from the dead "has never been observed, in any age or country," which does indeed assume the very point in dispute.

While it is fair game to point out these slips on Hume's part, this response doesn't grapple with the more defensible reading of his overall argument, which is less obviously question begging. That argument centers on the *proper weighing of evidence* and the *proportioning of belief* to the overall weight of evidence. Hume's contention is that since our own experience uniformly supports unexceptional laws of nature, we have the strongest possible evidence against any reported event that violates those laws. We have what Hume calls proof, as opposed to mere probability.[8] Even if testimonial evidence could amount to proof—a supposition Hume grants in part 1, but argues against in part 2—it couldn't in principle overturn the proof provided by uniform experience, which it would have to do for the testimony to be credible.

The fundamental flaw in Hume's argument lies in his distinction between proof and probability, and the associated claim that uniform experience of paired events (e.g., deaths not being followed by resurrections) furnish us with proof, rather than mere probability. As Hume defines proof, it constitutes the strongest possible evidence, which cannot in principle be overturned. In terms of probability theory, where the probability of an event can be expressed on a numerical range from 0 (no chance of the event occurring) to 1 (no chance of the event *not* occurring), Hume is asserting that the probability that any future event will conform to our past uniform experience is equal to 1. Otherwise, there would be no categorical distinction between proof and mere probability, between what is miraculous and what is merely marvelous (*EHU* 10.11).

This is a blunder in probabilistic reasoning. The laws of nature are established on the basis of inductive reasoning, and (as Hume was well aware) such reasoning cannot establish absolutely certain conclusions, i.e., conclusions with a probability of 1. It is true that the more uniform one's experiences are, the higher the probability that one's future experiences will replicate those past experiences, but no amount of experiences can rule out the possibility of a nonconforming future experience. Once this is recognized, Hume's proof/probability and miracle/marvel distinctions collapse, and the argument of part 1 of "Of Miracles" evaporates.

8. Scholars have noted an ambiguity in Hume's argument as to whether the uniform experience in question is to be understood as that of an individual or that of a peer group. My critique here can be applied to either interpretation.

John Earman captures the naivete of Hume's argument in one short paragraph:

> So here in a nutshell is Hume's first argument against miracles. A (Hume) miracle is a violation of a presumptive law of nature. By Hume's straight rule of induction, experience confers a probability of 1 on a presumptive law. Hence, the probability of a miracle is flatly zero. Very simple. And very crude. This "proof" works not only against resurrections but against, say, the "miracle" of a violation of the presumptive law of conservation of energy. Little wonder then that those of Hume's contemporaries who had a less crude view of how induction works found no merit in Hume's "proof."[9]

This exposes a closely related problem with Hume's argument against miracles: if sound, it would prove too much. It would utterly stultify scientific investigation, because no future observations could be accepted as evidence against a presumptive law of nature; in other words, there could never be rational grounds for revising our understanding of the laws of nature. For the consistent Humean, neither relativity theory nor quantum mechanics should have been accepted by physicists.

Indeed, Hume's argument entails that we should sometimes disbelieve the immediate testimony of our own senses. Suppose I have observed a thousand swans, and on every occasion the swans were white. In Humean terms, I have proof that all swans are white; based on my uniform experience, the probability that all swans are white is 1. Thus, if one day I observe—or seem to observe—a black swan before my very eyes, I should sooner conclude that I am dreaming or hallucinating than

9. John Earman, *Hume's Abject Failure: The Argument against Miracles* (New York: Oxford University Press, 2000), 23–24. "A (Hume) miracle" is Earman's way of referring to a miracle as defined by Hume.

that there really are some black swans. This is absurd enough in itself to suggest that there is something fishy about Hume's reasoning.

As numerous commentators have pointed out, we should be very suspicious of an argument that tells us we can immediately discount any claim that a miracle has occurred without seriously investigating the evidence offered in its support. As long as miracles are not flat-out impossible (which Hume has to concede), we must be open to considering that the overall evidence could justify accepting such a claim. Moreover, we already know that sometimes testimonial evidence is more than sufficient to justify the belief that a highly improbable event has occurred. Take the case of a lottery with ten million tickets sold. The odds of any one ticket winning are ten million to one. But if someone you knew told you that she had won the lottery, and her testimony was confirmed by other friends who had seen her ticket and checked her numbers against the winning numbers posted on the lottery website, you would not be irrational to believe it had happened.

This leads to a further point. Hume's argument, by its very design, discounts the cumulative evidential value of multiple, independent testimonies. If no testimonial evidence could in principle justify believing that someone had risen from the dead, the number of witnesses would be irrelevant. But once we grant that a resurrection has a nonzero probability, the number of witnesses becomes extremely relevant. In fact, Charles Babbage (1791–1871) proved mathematically that no matter how low the probability of an occurrence may be, provided that the probability is above zero and the independent witnesses testifying to the occurrence are minimally reliable (i.e., each witness's testimony is more likely to be true than false), there will always be some number N such that if the number of witnesses exceeds N, then the probability that every testimony is false is lower than the probability of the occurrence itself.[10] As Babbage pointed out, there can be no shortcuts: if we are to follow Hume's evidentialist maxim, we must consider the actual probabilities involved. But once we begin to plug numbers into the probability equations, we quickly see that Hume's sweeping claims don't have a leg to stand on.

All that aside, from a Reformed perspective, there is another aspect to the evidence for the resurrection of Christ that has been overlooked. Hume assumes throughout his argument that the testimony to the resurrection is merely human testimony. But this is a *de facto* denial of the Reformed Christian worldview. The testimony that believers rely upon today as the basis for their faith in the resurrection comes from the words of Christ and his apostles preserved in the New Testament, which is part of divinely inspired Scripture. Although Scripture has multiple human authors, it also has one divine author, the Holy Spirit (2 Tim. 3:16–17; 2 Peter 1:21). Christians believe the truths proclaimed in the New Testament because the Bible as a whole bears the marks of divine inspiration, and because by the internal witness of the Holy Spirit we recognize it to be the very Word of God. As the first chapter of the Westminster Confession of Faith puts it:

4. The authority of the Holy Scripture, for which it ought to be believed, and obeyed, dependeth not upon the testimony of any man, or church; but wholly upon God (who is truth itself) the author thereof: and therefore it is to be received, because it is the Word of God.

5. We may be moved and induced by the testimony of the church to an high and reverent esteem of the Holy

10. Charles Babbage, "On Hume's Argument against Miracles," in *The Ninth Bridgewater Treatise*, 2nd ed. (London: John Murray, 1838).

Scripture. And the heavenliness of the matter, the efficacy of the doctrine, the majesty of the style, the consent of all the parts, the scope of the whole (which is, to give all glory to God), the full discovery it makes of the only way of man's salvation, the many other incomparable excellencies, and the entire perfection thereof, are arguments whereby it doth abundantly evidence itself to be the Word of God: yet notwithstanding, our full persuasion and assurance of the infallible truth and divine authority thereof, is from the inward work of the Holy Spirit bearing witness by and with the Word in our hearts.

If this understanding of the Bible is correct, our evidence for believing in the resurrection isn't merely human testimony; it is divine testimony, which surely constitutes the strongest possible evidence. Once more we find Hume begging the question against the Reformed Christian by simply assuming that the testimony to the resurrection is no different than the testimony associated with any other alleged miracle.

Two final criticisms may be leveled at Hume's argument before we move on to other matters. The first was discussed earlier: Hume's evidentialist principle, which serves as the lynchpin of his argument, is falsified by numerous counterexamples and turns out to be self-defeating. The idea that "a wise man proportions his belief to the evidence" is not something that Hume, or anyone else, believes in proportion to the evidence that can be offered in its support.

The second criticism is that Hume's own skepticism about probabilistic reasoning undermines his entire argument. Hume argues elsewhere (*EHU* 4) that no matter how many times one observes a B-type event following an A-type event, one would never have rational grounds for believing that in the future all (or even most) A-type events will be followed by B-type events.

Just replace "A-type" with "death," and "B-type" with "non-resurrection," and the problem should be obvious. Far from providing insuperable evidence against miracles, our uniform experience of the regularity of nature provides no evidence against miracles—at least by Hume's own lights. Ironically, in his treatment of miracles, Hume turns out to be insufficiently skeptical.

The deeper irony is that Hume's argument against miracles depends on a conception of natural laws that his broader philosophy simply cannot support. Hume poses as a champion of science over religion, but his naturalistic worldview is destructive of both. In contrast, the Christian worldview can account, not only for the reality and knowability of natural laws, but also for the possibility of purposeful exceptions to those laws. Both laws and miracles—the ordinary and the extraordinary—presuppose the providence of God.

8

HUME AND CHRISTIAN APOLOGETICS

Hume was no ally of the Christian faith. His life's work may be viewed as a sustained attack on the reasonableness of Christian beliefs and the idea that Christianity provides the necessary foundations for morality and an orderly society. Nevertheless, in some important respects, Hume is an unwitting apologist for a biblical worldview. In this chapter, we will sketch out three areas in which Hume's arguments provide invaluable material for Christian apologetics. While the discussion here will be highly compressed, it will at least indicate the extent to which Hume's skepticism can be co-opted for more edifying purposes.

The Skeptical Sinkhole of Empiricism

Bertrand Russell considered Hume "one of the most important among philosophers, because he developed to its logical conclusion the empirical philosophy of Locke and Berkeley, and by making it self-consistent made it incredible."[1] Russell was quite correct. Although Hume's philosophy is a dead end, it is nonetheless valuable for exposing the implications of a consistent empiricism, although even Hume was less than fully consistent in his skeptical conclusions.

As Hume recognized, pure reason—that faculty by which we recognize the logical relations between ideas and propositions— cannot deliver concrete facts about the world. The logical truth that all bachelors are unmarried tells us nothing about whether any bachelors actually exist in the world. To know any concrete facts, insists the strict empiricist, we must rely on sense experience. Only our senses can deliver factual information about the world. The snag, however, is that our immediate experience can only tell us what *is* the case. It cannot tell us what *will be* the case (future truths), what *must be* the case (necessary truths), or what *ought to be* the case (normative truths). Yet that rules out vast areas of knowledge—or, at least, what we commonly assume to be knowledge. For example, on a strict empiricist basis, we cannot know either laws of nature (e.g., that momentum *will be* conserved in a collision of two objects) or laws of morality (e.g., that we *ought to be* honest in our dealings with others).

The skeptical implications do not end there. At any moment in time, a strict empiricist can really know only two things: (1) that he is presently having certain experiences, and (2) whatever is logically entailed by his having those experiences. That's not much at all. The strict empiricist cannot claim to know (1) that there is an external world existing independently of his experiences, (2) that objects continue to exist when not perceived (or that they really exist at all), (3) that his future experiences of the world will resemble his past experiences, (4) that

1. Russell, *A History of Western Philosophy* (New York: Simon & Schuster, 1945), 659.

his memories convey reliable information about the past (or that there really is a past), or (5) that he himself persists through time as a subject of knowledge. In short, the strict empiricist can know practically nothing of any significance.

Humean empiricism is a sinkhole for skepticism, yet it is still naively held by many critics of the Christian faith today. How often are we told that a rational person should rely only on "logic and evidence" (where "evidence" is understood in narrowly empirical terms) in forming beliefs? On such a basis, science would have to be tossed into the same pit as religion.

The many problems faced by empiricism suggest a powerful critique of the worldview of *metaphysical naturalism*. According to metaphysical naturalism, the only things that exist are physical things.[2] There is nothing beyond the physical universe, and human beings are nothing more than physical organisms, the product of billions of years of naturalistic, evolutionary processes. This view of human beings naturally (as it were) invites an empiricist epistemology, for it implies that our brains are essentially biological computers fitted with input and output devices, the inputs coming entirely by way of our sensory organs and nervous system. (How else could external data get into our brains?) The notion of *a priori* factual information does not sit comfortably with a naturalist account of human origins. Yet, as Hume rightly understood, a consistent empiricism rules out any metaphysical knowledge, in which case empiricism undercuts metaphysical naturalism itself. In short, metaphysical naturalism implies an epistemology (empiricism) according to which it is rationally unjustifiable.

---

2. Some naturalists will allow room for nonphysical entities, but only on condition that their existence and properties can be fully explained in terms of underlying physical entities.

The Problem of Induction

Hume is widely credited for bringing to attention a particularly important philosophical puzzle known as *the problem of induction*. Consider the following statements:

- Salt dissolves in water.
- Our planet will rotate 360 degrees on its axis over the next 24 hours.
- A tennis ball released from a height will accelerate downward at a constant rate.

Most likely, you believe that all three of these propositions are at least probably true. But are those beliefs rationally justified? All three of them are based on a form of reasoning known as induction, whereby general conclusions are drawn by extrapolation from a series of particular observations. While those observations don't logically entail the general conclusions (i.e., they don't rule out the possibility of an exceptional event), most people assume that it is reasonable to formulate general laws of nature and make predictions about future events on the basis of a sufficiently large number of past observations. Scientific progress depends upon it.

Inductive reasoning rests on a substantive assumption about the world, namely, that nature is generally uniform across time and space. We assume that the laws of nature (if there are such laws) are basically the same at all locations and at all times, such that causal connections in our small region of the universe are representative of causal connections in other regions of the universe, and past observations serve as a reliable predictor of future observations. On what rational basis are we justified in making such a weighty metaphysical assumption? If it cannot be rationally defended, what does that imply about the rationality of our inductive inferences?

Hume recognized that our assumption of the uniformity of nature cannot be proven by pure reason. It isn't a logical truism, because there is no logical contradiction involved in denying the assumption (*EHU* 4.18). When people are asked why we should think that nature is uniform across time and space, the most common answer is that we have *observed* it to be uniform. When we have made predictions in the past based on that assumption, those predictions have usually turned out to be correct, and thus the assumption is vindicated. On the face of it, that seems like a reasonable answer, but Hume deftly exposes the fallacy at its heart:

> When a man says, *I have found, in all past instances, such sensible qualities conjoined with such secret powers*: And when he says, *similar sensible qualities will always be conjoined with similar secret powers*, he is not guilty of a tautology, nor are these propositions in any respect the same. You say that the one proposition is an inference from the other. But you must confess that the inference is not intuitive; neither is it demonstrative: Of what nature is it then? To say it is experimental [i.e., based on experience—JNA], is begging the question. For all inferences from experience suppose, as their foundation, that the future will resemble the past, and that similar powers will be conjoined with similar sensible qualities. If there be any suspicion, that the course of nature may change, and that the past may be no rule for the future, all experience becomes useless, and can give rise to no inference or conclusion. It is impossible, therefore, that any arguments from experience can prove this resemblance of the past to the future; since all these arguments are founded on the supposition of that resemblance. (EHU 4.21)

Hume's point is simply this: It is fallacious, circular reasoning to appeal to past experiences in order to justify inferences from past experiences to future experiences. It is question begging to justify the reliability of inductive inferences by way of an inductive inference (i.e., extrapolating from past inductions to future inductions).

The epistemological problem exposed by Hume has proven remarkably difficult to solve on a naturalistic basis, and it continues to be hotly debated by philosophers—not least by philosophers of science, for whom it is especially unsettling. One popular approach is to appeal to the criterion of *simplicity*: all else being equal, simpler hypotheses are more likely to be correct, and the uniformity of nature is a simpler hypothesis than its denial. The trouble with this response is that it merely transforms the problem into a new one, namely, the problem of justifying the criterion of simplicity, which—like the assumption of uniformity—cannot be proven on the basis of experience without begging the question.

How then can our assumption of the uniformity of nature be justified? How can we account for the rationality of induction? It seems that only an omniscient being could enjoy direct knowledge of the uniformity of nature across space and time. The God revealed to us in the Bible is a God of order (1 Cor. 14:33), who created the natural world and exercises sovereign control over it (Gen. 1:1; Isa. 42:5; 45:12; 48:13). He knows that nature is uniform precisely because he is the author of nature and continually sustains it (Jer. 31:35–36). Furthermore, God is the creator of human beings, including our cognitive faculties, which allow us to "think God's thoughts after him"; our inductive inferences are reliable precisely because God has designed them to be reliable. For those who hold to a Christian worldview, with its robust doctrine of creation and revelational epistemology, the problem of induction is really no problem at all.

Russell lamented that if Hume's problem of induction cannot be solved, "there is no intellectual difference between sanity and insanity."[3] Such is the fate of those who deny the God who has clearly revealed himself through the natural order (Rom. 1:18–21).

A Hume-Inspired Transcendental Argument

The problem of induction may be viewed as a particular instance of a more general epistemological problem. Is there any rational order to the facts of the world, and, if so, how can we have epistemic access to that rational order? How can the multifarious facts of experience be rationally connected, so as to give us genuine knowledge of the world and its operations?

Hume's answer, in effect, is that such knowledge is impossible. Given his starting point, his answer is correct. Kant considered this a philosophical scandal, even though he agreed with Hume that all factual knowledge of the world must come through sense experience. Kant's innovative response to Hume's skepticism was his "Copernican revolution" in epistemology: although we cannot know the world as it is in itself, we can know the world as it appears to us, because our minds impose rational order on the data of experience. Kant called his theory "transcendental idealism," but we might just as well call it *anthropocentric antirealism*, for, on Kant's view, the world of experience—the world we take ourselves to inhabit—isn't a mind-independent reality, but rather a construction of the active human mind.

Kant's system, while ingenious in its own way, fails to provide a satisfactory answer to the problems raised by Hume. Not only is it internally inconsistent (Kant couldn't avoid making some positive claims about the unknowable noumenal world), but, like all forms of antirealism, it is haunted by the specter of epistemological relativism. If the world is a construction of the human

---

3. Russell, *A History of Western Philosophy*, 673.

mind, which human mind is doing the constructing? How can I be sure that the rational order I impose upon my experience is the same for everyone? Kant was the champion of intellectual autonomy—human reason must serve as the supreme judge— yet the existence of seven billion minds on earth implies seven billion independent and competing authorities.

As a child of the Enlightenment, Kant had faith in universal reason, the idea that the rational principles and structuring concepts of the human mind must be the same for all. Indeed, he endeavored to demonstrate it by way of a *transcendental argument*, a distinctive type of argument that seeks to expose the necessary preconditions of human knowledge. What must be the case for knowledge to be possible? What must be the case for the empirical world to be rationally intelligible?

Kant thought he could show by this type of argumentation that the principles and concepts we use to order our experience could not have been otherwise: they are necessary, and therefore must be universal. His reasoning on this point, however, is notoriously obscure and hard to reconstruct. In any event, his conclusions seem quite mistaken. There is no apparent reason why the laws of nature, such as Newton's laws of motion, couldn't have been different. Indeed, pure reason doesn't demand that there be any causal laws at all. Even space itself could have been four-dimensional rather than three-dimensional; there is nothing logically or mathematically incoherent about such a scenario.

Underlying all this is a methodology that appears to beg the question. To avoid the abyss of relativism, Kant needs to show by pure *a priori* reasoning that everyone rationally orders their experiences according to the same basic principles and concepts. Yet his arguments are the product of one particular intellect. Kant's conclusions may be rational by the light of his own reason, but why must they be rational to everyone else? His methodology presupposes the very thing at stake, namely, universal reason.

In the end, Kant doesn't so much answer Hume's skeptical challenge as seek to subvert it by redefining "the world"— internalizing it, and making it a product of human cognition rather than (as common sense suggests) a mind-independent reality. But his attempts to stave off relativism must be judged a failure. Any epistemology that makes man the measure of all things is built on sinking sand.

The Reformed philosopher Cornelius Van Til advocated a very different response to Hume's skepticism. Van Til argued that Kant was asking the right questions, but offering the wrong answers. Adapting Kant's transcendental method in the service of Christian apologetics, Van Til argued that the true alternative to skepticism is not an anthropocentric antirealism, but rather a *theocentric realism*. We must presuppose God, not ourselves, as the ultimate rationality and the ultimate authority. God is the "All-Conditioner," the Personal Absolute who creates and orders all things according to his perfect wisdom and sovereign will. On this view, God is the authoritative pre-interpreter of the world, and as creatures made in God's image, we are designed to be reinterpreters of God's world. God's knowledge is original and constructive; ours is derivative and reconstructive. Human knowledge is possible because of an *analogical* relationship between God's mind and our minds, between God's reason and our reason. Genuine knowledge of the world—of the world as it really is—is possible only if (1) the facts of the world are ordered "from above," and (2) our minds are configured "from above" to order the facts of experience in the same way.[4]

We can put the matter in terms of what Kant considered to be the crucial question: How is synthetic *a priori* knowledge

4. Cornelius Van Til, *A Survey of Christian Epistemology* (Nutley, NJ: Presbyterian & Reformed, 1977), 216–18; James N. Anderson, "If Knowledge Then God: The Epistemological Theistic Arguments of Plantinga and Van Til," *Calvin Theological Journal* 40 (2005): 49–75.

possible? How is it possible to know substantive facts about the world apart from sense experience?

Hume's answer: It isn't possible, so we must learn to live with skepticism.

Kant's answer: We must posit that the world we experience is a construction of the autonomous human mind—although, in the end (in agreement with Hume), we cannot know the world as such, as it is in itself.

Van Til's answer: We must posit that the world is the creation of a rational God and that humans are designed to think God's thoughts after him. Synthetic *a priori* knowledge of the world is possible for us only because it ultimately derives from God's knowledge. God knows the world directly and exhaustively. He knows that nature is uniform, that objects persist through time, that every event has a causal explanation, and that our perceptual faculties provide reliable epistemic access to an external world. God knows these things because he *ordained* them. But God has also designed the human mind to naturally and non-inferentially believe these things—indeed, to take them for granted. Since these basic beliefs are not the product of mere chance or blind natural processes, but rather the product of divine design, they are rationally well-grounded. What could be more rational than the intuitions of a mind created and ordered by God? What Hume could only credit to nature and custom, devoid of reason, the Christian will gladly and gratefully credit to God.

It has been said that orthodoxy owes a debt to heresy. If Pelagius unwittingly served the cause of Christian theology, Hume unwittingly served the cause of Christian apologetics. Even though his philosophical project must be judged a failure, it is a highly instructive failure, for it exposes the irrationalism of a naturalistic worldview founded on the autonomy of the human mind. When one encounters a dead end, the only reasonable course of action is to turn around and head in the opposite direction.

EPILOGUE

THE HUMEAN PREDICAMENT

A hundred yards downhill from the statue of David Hume on Edinburgh's Royal Mile is St Giles' Cathedral, also known as the High Kirk of Edinburgh. Inside that historic church stands another statue, that of John Knox, the famous leader of the Scottish Reformation. The two statues represent two worldviews at war in the West today. The first represents the secular, naturalistic, antireligious worldview that dominates the academic world, both the sciences and the humanities—a worldview that champions human autonomy and seeks to explain human nature without any reference to God or divine revelation. The second represents an orthodox Christian worldview that acknowledges the triune God as the sovereign Creator and governor of the universe, the Bible as his authoritative verbal revelation, and humans as creatures made in their Creator's image, fallen and corrupted by sin, but forgiven and renewed by God's grace through faith in the person and work of Jesus Christ.

By and large, the academic world today stands with Hume, as do many churches that once held to the doctrines proclaimed by Knox.[1] Although Hume's secular vision is celebrated and embraced by public intellectuals, relatively few acknowledge the self-defeating implications of his worldview. To be a true disciple of Hume, one must ultimately renounce not only religion, but also science and common sense. Nevertheless, an uncompromising secularism continues to make headway in Western culture under the banner of "reason and science," pushing historical Christian beliefs and practices to the margins.

If the West is to be saved, a new Reformation is needed: not merely a theological and ecclesiastical reformation, but an epistemological and cultural reformation. Hume must decrease; Christ must increase. *Kyrie eleison.*

---

1. A 2009 survey asked 1,800 academic philosophers which nonliving philosopher they most identified with. The top answer, by a clear margin, was Hume (trailed by Aristotle and Kant). See https://philpapers.org/surveys/.

GLOSSARY

Italicized entries are terms defined according to Hume's particular usage.

a posteriori. Subsequent to, or based upon, sense experience. See also *a priori.*

a priori. Prior to, or independent of, sense experience. See also *a posteriori.*

analytic. Pertaining to a conceptual or logical truism, such as "All cats are mammals." In Hume's terminology, pertaining to a "relation of ideas." See also *synthetic.*

antirealism. The view that there is no such thing as a "real world" that exists and has the features it has, independently of the human mind—or, if there is such a thing, it is unknowable. On this view, the world that we experience is, in some nontrivial sense, a construction of the human mind. See also *realism.*

beg the question. To reason in a circle or assume the very point needing to be proven. Example: "I know I'm not just a brain in a vat, because I can see my arms and legs!"

causation. The concept or relation of cause and effect, which philosophers have found excruciatingly difficult to define and analyze. Roughly, the notion of bringing about a change or effect, perhaps by means of inherent powers or potentialities.

cosmological argument. An argument for the existence of God, according to which there must exist a transcendent first cause that ultimately explains the existence of the universe and/or effects within the universe.

empiricism. The doctrine that knowledge must be grounded in immediate sense experience.

epistemic. Relating to belief or knowledge.

evidentialism. The doctrine that beliefs are rationally justified only if they are based on sufficient evidence.

henotheism. The worship of one god while allowing for the existence of other gods.

idea. A less lively and vivid perception; a mental copy of an original *impression*. See also *impression*.

imagination. One of the two faculties (the other being *memory*) that produce *ideas*. According to Hume, the ideas formed by the imagination may be products of either *reason* or *fancy*.

impression. A more lively and vivid perception; a feeling as opposed to a thought. See also *idea*.

induction. A common form of reasoning by which general conclusions are drawn from a series of particular instances or observations.

logical positivism. A philosophical movement in the early twentieth century that advocated a strict empiricism and a verificationist theory of meaning (i.e., a statement is meaningful only if it is true by definition or verifiable by empirical observation).

metaphysical naturalism. The philosophical doctrine that only "natural" entities exist, that the space-time cosmos is the only reality.

methodological naturalism. A method of inquiry (in science, history, or any other field) that restricts explanations to "natural" entities and laws.

monotheism. The belief in (and worship of) one God.

noumenal. In Kant's philosophy, pertaining to the world as it is "in itself," apart from experience. See also *phenomenal*.

ontological argument. An argument for the existence of God, according to which God's existence is entailed by his perfection. The basic idea is that God's necessary existence is "contained in" the very definition of God, and thus it is logically contradictory to deny God's existence.

passion. A secondary, reflective *impression* that moves us toward actions.

perception. Any item of mental content or present experience, such as a thought or a feeling.

phenomenal. In Kant's philosophy, pertaining to the world as it appears to us in our experience. See also *noumenal*.

polytheism. The belief in (and worship of) many gods.

primary quality. An attribute that exists in the object itself (e.g., the roundness of an apple). See also *secondary quality*.

rationalism. The doctrine that knowledge must be grounded in undeniable or self-evident truths of reason. Alternatively, the doctrine that all truth claims must be tested and vindicated by human reason.

realism. The commonsense view that there is a "real world" that exists and has the features it has independently of the human mind. On this view, for example, "Mount Everest is the highest mountain on the planet" is true, regardless of what anyone thinks or experiences. See also *antirealism*.

secondary quality. An attribute that exists only in the mind of the perceiver and not in the object itself (e.g., the redness of an apple). See also *primary quality*.

synthetic. Pertaining to a nonanalytic proposition expressing some factual or substantive claim about the world, such as "The cat is on the mat." In Hume's terminology, pertaining to a "matter of fact." See also *analytic.*

teleological argument. An argument for the existence of God, based on the order and apparent design and purpose in the universe.

utilitarianism. A theory of ethics, according to which morally good actions are those that result in the most pleasure and the least pain for the most people ("the greatest happiness for the greatest number").

virtue (vice). A character trait or disposition that is perceived as morally good (bad).

understanding. The faculty of reason by which we make either demonstrative (deductive) or probabilistic inferences.

RECOMMENDED READING

If you read only one work by Hume, it should be *An Enquiry concerning Human Understanding* (1748, 1777), which serves as a reasonably concise, self-contained introduction to his philosophical project. Follow that with *An Enquiry concerning the Principles of Morals* (1751, 1777) and *Dialogues concerning Natural Religion* (1779). The adventurous may then be steeled to wade through the three volumes of *A Treatise of Human Nature* (1739–40). Finally, *My Own Life* (1777) offers Hume's self-assessment at the end of his career.

Hume's entire corpus is in the public domain and available on the website davidhume.org.

The following secondary sources will also be useful for understanding the strengths and weaknesses of Hume's thought:

Blackburn, Simon. *How to Read Hume*. London: Granta Books, 2008. A short, accessible introduction to the contours of Hume's thought from a modern-day disciple who shares Hume's disdain for religion.

Earman, John. *Hume's Abject Failure: The Argument against Miracles*. New York: Oxford University Press, 2000. Part 1 offers a devastating critique of Hume's argument against reported miracles. Part 2 provides excerpts from prior works that influenced "Of Miracles" and subsequent works that responded to it.

Fogelin, Robert J. *A Defense of Hume on Miracles*. Princeton, NJ: Princeton University Press, 2003. Fogelin attempts to defend Hume's argument against miracles in response to the withering critiques by David Johnson and John Earman. See Timothy McGrew's review in *Mind* (vol. 114, issue 453, January 1, 2005) to understand why Fogelin's defense fails.

Garrett, Don. *Hume*. New York: Routledge, 2015. A thorough and largely sympathetic introduction from a highly regarded Hume scholar. Garrett works hard to bring out the subtleties of Hume's thought and to develop a coherent interpretation of his overall philosophy.

Geivett, R. Douglas, and Gary Habermas, eds. *In Defense of Miracles: A Comprehensive Case for God's Action in History*. Downers Grove, IL: InterVarsity Press, 1997. A collection of essays by Christian philosophers responding to Hume's arguments against miracles. Includes the full text of "Of Miracles" and a chapter by Antony Flew offering a "neo-Humean" case against miracles.

Harris, James A. *Hume: An Intellectual Biography*. Cambridge: Cambridge University Press, 2015. A comprehensive overview of Hume's life and work, providing historical context to his various writings.

Millican, Peter, ed. *Reading Hume on Human Understanding: Essays on the First Enquiry*. Oxford: Clarendon Press, 2002. An extensive analysis from a pantheon of Hume scholars.

Norton, David Fate, and Jacqueline Taylor, eds. *The Cambridge Companion to Hume*. 2nd ed. Cambridge: Cambridge

University Press, 2009. A collection of scholarly essays on all major aspects of Hume's thought. A helpful companion to the primary sources.

Russell, Paul, ed. *The Oxford Handbook of Hume.* Oxford: Oxford University Press, 2016. Oxford's counterpart to Cambridge's *Companion*, with twice as many chapters and analyses on the more critical side.

Sennett, James F., and Douglas Groothuis, eds. *In Defense of Natural Theology: A Post-Humean Assessment.* Downers Grove, IL: InterVarsity Press, 2005. A follow-up to the 1997 Geivett-Habermas volume. The contributors defend the traditional arguments for the existence of God against Hume's objections and challenge the epistemology on which Hume's critique is founded.

Stroud, Barry. *Hume.* London: Routledge & Kegan Paul, 1977. A groundbreaking interpretation and critical analysis of Hume's philosophy that has provoked much subsequent discussion. Stroud is charitable yet penetrating in his criticisms.

Yandell, Keith E. *Hume's "Inexplicable Mystery": His Views on Religion.* Philadelphia: Temple University Press, 1990. A detailed exposition and critique of *NHR* and *DNR* by a Christian philosopher.

In addition, the online *Stanford Encyclopedia of Philosophy* (https://plato.stanford.edu) contains a number of peer-reviewed scholarly articles on Hume's philosophy that serve as useful introductions and guides to the (extensive) secondary literature.

INDEX OF SUBJECTS
AND NAMES

James N. Anderson (PhD, PhD, University of Edinburgh) is the Carl W. McMurray Professor of Theology and Philosophy at Reformed Theological Seminary, Charlotte, and an ordained minister in the Associate Reformed Presbyterian Church. He specializes in Reformed philosophical theology and apologetics, with a particular focus on the presuppositionalism of Cornelius Van Til. He is the author of *Paradox in Christian Theology* (2007), *What's Your Worldview?* (2014), and *Why Should I Believe Christianity?* (2016). His writings and lectures on various topics in Christian theology, philosophy, ethics, and apologetics can be found online at www.proginosko.com.

He has a long-standing concern to bring the Reformed theological tradition into greater dialogue with contemporary analytic philosophy. Before studying philosophy, he also earned a PhD in Computer Simulation from the University of Edinburgh. He is a member of the Society of Christian Philosophers, the British Society for the Philosophy of Religion, and the Evangelical Philosophical Society. Prior to joining RTS Charlotte, he served as an assistant pastor at the historic Charlotte Chapel in Edinburgh where he engaged in regular preaching, teaching, and pastoral ministry.

He is married to Catriona, and they have three children. Outside of work, he enjoys hiking and running, reading techno-thrillers, writing software, and watching Christopher Nolan movies.

ALSO FROM P&R PUBLISHING

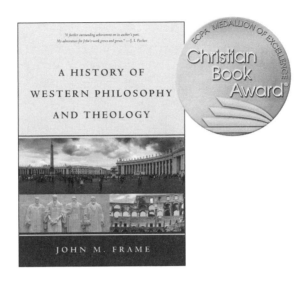

**Winner of the 2017 ECPA Gold Medallion Award
in the Bible Reference Works Category**

A History of Western Philosophy and Theology is the fruit of John Frame's forty-five years of teaching philosophical subjects. No other survey of the history of Western thought offers the same invigorating blend of expositional clarity, critical insight, and biblical wisdom. The supplemental study questions, bibliographies, links to audio lectures, quotes from influential thinkers, twenty appendices, and indexed glossary make this an excellent main textbook choice for seminary- and college-level courses and for personal study.

"This is the most important book ever written on the major figures and movements in philosophy. We have needed a sound guide, and this is it."
    —**Vern S. Poythress,** Professor of New Testament, Westminster
    Theological Seminary